Saladmaster®

Healthy and Nutritious Cooking

Published by Saladmaster, Inc., in association with Leisure Time Publishing, a division of Heritage Worldwide, Inc., 9029 Directors Row, Dallas, Texas 75247.

Pictured on front cover: Parmesan Perch (page 74).

Photography: David Barnett, The Sugar Association, American Mushroom Institute, Rice Council of America, National Turkey Federation, National Livestock & Meat Board, American Dairy Association, International Banana Association, National Pecan Marketing Council, National Broiler Council.

First Printing.

Manufactured in the United States of America.

Contents

Quality Features

★ Multi-radiant core for even heat distribution ... bottom and sides.
★ Dripless pouring edge means no messy dribbles down the side of pan.
★ Cool pistol-grip handle for safer handling.
★ Vapor seal cover locks in nutrition and enhances flavor.
★ Permanent electric weld construction for ease of cleaning.
★ Rounded corners prevent food and grease build-up ... makes cleaning quick and easy.
★ Heat-shielded knobs and stainless flame guard for safe and easy handling.
★ Vapo-Valve warning signal prevents burning and helps preserve nutrition.
★ Self-storing lids and stainless steel hang-up rings.
★ Highest quality stainless steel mirror finish ... easy to keep like new for years and years.
★ You'll never have to buy another set of cookware ... you now own the best.

Welcome...

to the wonderful world of *Saladmaster Healthy and Nutritious Cooking* ...and congratulations on becoming an owner of the finest cookware available.

Saladmaster FIVE-STAR stainless steel cooking utensils are the finest quality products on the market today. Together, they provide a system of waterless and greaseless food preparation which enhances food flavor while retaining its nutritional value ... allowing you to serve better meals, more economically, without diluting natural vitamins and minerals.

The unique multi-layer construction of Saladmaster cookware features radiant heat conducting inner layers of aluminum alloys and outer layers of stainless steel for optimum heat distribution. This design allows you to cook with minimum heat ... saving dollars on your energy bill. The patented Vapo-Valve eliminates guesswork and signals when to turn down heat. The vapor seal cover creates a semi-vacuum which shortens cooking time while using a lower temperature setting.

Saladmaster quality is evident in every facet of utensil design. Cool pistol-grip handles, heat shield knobs and a dripless pouring edge make serving easier. Clean-up is minimized by rounded corners, which prevent food build-up. High-quality TP304 stainless steel retains its brilliant appearance for many years. Even storage is easier with stainless steel hang-up rings and self-storing lids.

Most important is the Saladmaster guarantee of quality ... a lifetime warranty which ensures your cookware will be free from defects in material and workmanship for as long as you own them. By following the instructions for use and care of your Saladmaster cookware, you will enjoy years of economical, healthier and more nutritious cooking for you and your family.

The recipes and information provided in this cookbook have been produced to make it easy for you to prepare foods without using grease and water. The material included covers a wide range of menu selections ... developed by Saladmaster "chefs" throughout the world ... using FIVE-STAR cookware and the original Saladmaster Food Processor. We sincerely hope that you will enjoy the healthy and nutritious method of Saladmaster food preparation ... and that you will adapt your own favorite recipes to the wonderful world of Saladmaster cooking!

Saladmaster®

Care and Use Instructions

Before First Use

Thoroughly wash your new Saladmaster cookware in hot, soapy water containing 1 cup vinegar per gallon of water. This removes all traces of manufacturing oils and polishing compounds . . . preparing your cooking utensils for daily use. Rinse in clear, hot water and dry well with a clean towel.

After Each Use

Your easy-care stainless steel cookware normally requires only washing in hot, soapy water after each use . . . rinse and dry.

If your new utensils turn bluish on the interior, re-wash thoroughly with vinegar and hot soapy water to remove balance of factory oils and polishing compounds. During the first month of use, you may also notice a white residue in the bottom of a utensil. This is a normal occurrence, which diminishes with use and which can be easily removed with Saladmaster Glo that comes packed with your cookware. Simply rinse out the utensil with hot water and drain off all excess water leaving only a few drops. In this remaining moisture, sprinkle a small amount of Salad-master Glo to make a "paste." Using a paper towel, gently rub the discolored area in a circular motion. Rinse well in hot water to remove all cleanser, dry with clean towel. This procedure will also remove any brownish carbon deposit which may appear on the outside of your utensil when cooking over gas . . . or when a golden brown or blue heat tint results from persistent overheating.

To preserve the high-polish exterior finish on all utensils and covers, avoid the use of steel wool or harsh abrasives which will scratch the surface. To clean, spread Saladmaster Glo on a damp cloth or paper towel and rub the utensil in a circular motion until shiny. Wash, rinse, dry.

Persistent overheating or removing cover during cooking may cause food to burn or stick. To remove residue resulting from dried food or meat drippings, partially fill utensil with water. Heat to boil for a few minutes; let stand until cool. Discard water; loosen food with wooden utensil, if necessary. Rub with Saladmaster Glo cleanser; wash, rinse, dry. Always make certain no food is lodged inside the Vapo-Valve in the cover. Also, be sure that the rim remains clean and free of foods. This is very important in obtaining the proper sealing of the cover onto the utensil.

Heat Settings

When cooking with most Saladmaster FIVE-STAR utensils, never use a heat setting greater than medium. The special Vapo-Valve cannot function properly if high heat is used, and no natural moisture will form inside.

Most of the recipes included herein begin at medium heat. When the Vapo-Valve begins to "click" steadily, you must immediately reduce heat until the valve stops clicking. On an electric stove, medium heat is the halfway point between the highest and lowest markings. Please note that this point does not necessarily fall at the "Medium" marking of all electric stoves. For best results, follow the definition of medium heat described above. On a gas range, medium heat is a flame low enough so that you can comfortably hold your hand six inches above the flame, to a count of ten. After the Vapo-Valve "clicks," reduce to a low heat setting . . . where your hand can be held one inch above the flame.

All metals are affected by high heat or extreme changes in temperature which cause the metal to warp. **Do not** put a hot utensil in contact with cold water. Even as thick and heavy as Saladmaster cookware is, there is a possibility you may warp it. Let the utensil cool down and always add warm water. If the utensil warps, it is not covered by the Saladmaster Limited Lifetime Warranty.

Preheating

For best results, follow these simple guidelines:

When cooking fruits and vegetables, rinse them in cold water in the pan you plan to use. Drain well, and follow the instructions in the recipe. Remember, damage to the vitamin and mineral content of the vegetable occurs in the first three to four minutes of cooking time.

When cooking meats, start with a hot, dry pan. We suggest placing a piece of paper towel in the bottom of the pan or skillet. Warm at medium heat. When the paper becomes golden brown, the utensil is preheated. Carefully remove paper towel and proceed with instructions in the recipe.

Steam Cooking

Your steamer inset is the motor of your Saladmaster cookware set. Use the 3-qt sauce pan and fill with 4 cups water ... about ½" below where the bottom of the steamer inset will sit. Bring water to a boil over medium heat. After water is boiling, place food in steamer. Insert the steamer into sauce pan; cover and steam until food is tender/crisp. (Periodically check/add water resulting from evaporation.)

Combination and Stack Cooking

Combination and stack cooking are time, money and energy-saving features of Saladmaster FIVE-STAR cookware. The thick, five-ply construction is a superb heat conductor because heat travels rapidly and uniformly across the bottom, up the sides, and around the cover to completely surround the food being cooked. That same heat-conducting power transmits uniform heat from utensil to utensil, making it possible to cook an entire meal on just one burner of the stove without losing or transmitting flavors. This is an advantageous slower cooking process that eliminates the possibility of overcooking.

Side-by-side cooking is also an advantageous way to use fewer utensils for one given menu. For example, cook fresh carrots next to frozen peas in one utensil. Remember, vitamins and minerals stay in the foods ... and flavors will not mix.

Vapo-Valve

Your curiosity to see how everything is cooking will be very strong at first, so go ahead and peek once or twice. Just be sure to spin the lid so that the Vapo-Valve "clicks," indicating that it has re-sealed itself. If it does not, increase heat until the valve "clicks" again, then reduce to low. If your range is so adjusted that the Vapo-Valve continues to click when you have reduced the heat as far as it will go, you may have to purchase a wire trivet (the type used under glass coffee pots on electric stoves) or an abestos heat displacing pad (the type used on gas stoves) to eliminate the problem of too much heat.

Water Seal for High Dome Cover

When roasting turkey, chicken, beef, pork or wild game in the Dutch oven, a water seal must form between the high dome cover and rim of the pan to assure tenderness and low shrinkage. Begin cooking over medium heat until bubbling occurs around the rim. Reduce heat gradually to low in order to retain moisture in the rim. There should always be a ring of water in the rim so the lid can float and spin freely. If the cover grates and drags, the water seal has been lost and it is necessary to raise the heat slowly until the water ring re-forms.

Roasting

Saladmaster cookware allows you to roast meat on top of the range at low heat ... without grease or water. By this range-top low heat method, shrinkage is reduced to a minimum and savings in fuel are made possible. One of the most important nutrients in meat ... protein ... is adversely affected by excessively high heat, making low heat cooking very important.

Preheat Dutch oven 3-4 minutes over medium heat (see "Preheating," page 2). Place meat firmly in Dutch oven without cover. Press down to assure even "searing." Brown over medium heat. Meat may stick but will loosen as browning continues. Turn meat and sear well on other side. Season meat according to taste and diet. Cover. When Vapo-Valve "clicks," reduce heat to low. Cook according to recipe instructions.

Stir-Fry Cooking

Your Saladmaster Wok is an "all-purpose" cooking utensil ... capable of preparing everything from wonderful stir-fry dishes to roasting a medium-size turkey. As such, you can generally use your wok just as you would a fry pan ... preparing all types of dishes without using grease or water.

The unique 5-ply construction of the Saladmaster Wok allows you to now stir-fry most vegetables and meats without the use of oil. By using fresh produce, poultry, fish and meat, food flavor, color, texture and nutritional value is retained.

Saladmaster Food Processor

The Saladmaster Food Processor is a precision engineered, superbly constructed kitchen aid that is quick and easy to assemble and use. It is heavily chrome plated and will not chip, peel, stain or pit. The five cones will not rust, dull or stain. It chops, peels, strings, waffles, grates, slices and shreds. Just insert food and turn the handle. Sets up quickly, cleans easily.

No. 1 SHREDDER
Grating or Shredding
Cheese, Coconut, Apples, Chocolate, Bananas, Cabbage, Onions, Hard Cooked Eggs, Celery, Nuts, Crackers.

No. 2 STRINGER
Cutting Medium Strings
Shoestring Potatoes, Julienned Vegetables for Combination Salads, Onions, Celery, Cheese, Shrimp, Fish, Apples, Fruits.

No. 3 FRENCH FRYER
Cutting Demi-French Size
Potatoes, Beets, Carrots, Parsnips, Turnips.

No. 4 THIN SLICER
Thin Slicing
Cabbage for Slaw or Sauerkraut, Potatoes for
Chips, Escalloped or Raw Fries, Nuts, Radishes,
Cucumbers, Carrots, Onions, Pickles, Zucchini.

No. 5 WAFFLER
Thicker Slicing
Potatoes, Apples, Beets, Bananas, Carrots, Zucchini,
Cucumbers, Cabbage.

Enjoy Your Saladmaster Cookware

Each of the recipes provided in this cookbook lists the Saladmaster utensils which are best suited for preparation of each dish. Cooking times and temperatures are calculated using this cookware . . . and may change accordingly should you use different utensils. In addition, many recipes exclude salt for dietary purposes. Should you desire, we suggest "seasoning to taste" after the food is prepared.

Learn to use your new utensils and you will love them. Should any questions or unusual situations develop . . . or if you have a helpful hint or favorite recipe to share with us . . . call or write your nearest Saladmaster Dealer immediately, or contact the home office . . . 912 - 113th Street, Arlington, Texas 76010.

Measurements and Conversions

Simplified Measures

3 teaspoons (tsp)	=	1 tablespoon (tbsp)
4 tablespoons (tbsp)	=	¼ cup
16 tablespoons (tbsp)	=	1 cup
2 cups	=	1 pint (pt)
2 pints (pt)	=	1 quart (qt)
4 quarts (qt)	=	1 gallon (gal)
8 ounces (oz)	=	1 cup
16 ounces (oz)	=	1 pound (lb)

Equivalents

Beef Broth
1 cup = 1 bouillon cube or 1 teaspoon instant granules plus 1 cup water

Cabbage
1 pound = 4½ cups shredded

Carrots
1 pound = 6 medium carrots = 3 cups shredded or sliced = 2½ cups diced

Garlic
1 medium garlic clove = ⅛ teaspoon garlic powder = ⅛ teaspoon minced garlic

Gingerroot
1 teaspoon fresh grated = ¼ teaspoon ground ginger (slightly different flavor)

Mushrooms
1 cup fresh sliced mushrooms = 1 can (4 ounces)

Onions
1 bunch green onions = 1 cup sliced onion
½ cup chopped onion = 1 teaspoon dried onion = 1 teaspoon onion powder

Bell Pepper
1 medium bell pepper = 1 cup chopped

Meat
1 pound = 3½ cups sliced = 3 cups minced = 2 cups ground

Pea Pods
6 ounces fresh = 1 (6 ounce) package frozen

Rice
1 cup raw, long-grain = 3 cups cooked rice
1 cup instant rice = 1-2 cups cooked rice
1 cup brown rice = 3-4 cups cooked rice

Zucchini
1 medium zucchini = 1 cup sliced

Appetizers & Snacks

Vegetable Dip

Utensil: 2-qt sauce pan

3 (8 oz) pkgs lite cream cheese
½ cup water
1 (10¾ oz) can tomato soup
1 (3 oz) pkg lemon jello
1 cup chopped bell pepper
½ cup chopped onion
½ cup chopped pecans
1 cup lite mayonnaise

In sauce pan mix cream cheese, water, soup and jello. Heat over medium-low until cheese melts. Remove from heat; stir in remaining ingredients. Chill overnight. Serve with fresh vegetables or chips.

Fresh Fruit Dip

Utensil: 2-qt stainless steel bowl

1 pt sour cream
3 tbsp powdered sugar
1½ tbsp Amaretto
1 tsp almond extract

Mix ingredients together in bowl. Serve with strawberries or other fresh fruit.

Texana Guacamole Dip

Utensil: 3-qt stainless steel bowl

2 avocados; peeled, mashed
4 oz lite cream cheese
2 tbsp minced onion
2 tsp salt or seasoning substitute
1 tsp chili powder
1 clove garlic; crushed
   Dash of Tabasco sauce
4 tsp lemon juice
2 medium tomatoes; peeled, chopped

Combine all ingredients in bowl. Cover; chill 1 hour. Serve with taco chips.

Ranch Bean Dip

Utensils: 1-qt sauce pan, 2-qt stainless steel bowl, Saladmaster Food Processor

1 medium onion
1¼ cups sharp Cheddar cheese
1 (1 lb) can ranch-style beans
4 jalapeno peppers; chopped
1 tbsp jalapeno pepper juice
1 clove garlic; minced
1 tsp chili powder

Cut onion using #2 Stringer food processor cone. Grate cheese using #1 Shredder cone.

Process beans in blender or bowl using electric mixer. Mix beans and all other ingredients together in uncovered sauce pan. Heat over medium-low until cheese melts. Serve with corn chips.

Cocktail Meatballs

Utensils: Electric skillet, 3-qt stainless steel bowl

1   tbsp cooking sherry
1   tbsp lite soy sauce
⅛   tsp sesame seed oil
¼   cup water
½   clove garlic; minced
½   tsp ground ginger
1   lb lean ground beef

In bowl combine sherry, soy sauce, sesame seed oil, water, garlic and ginger. Add ground beef; mix together thoroughly. Form into balls about 1" in diameter.

Preheat electric skillet at 350°. Place meatballs in skillet; cook uncovered 10 minutes. Turn meatballs; cook 5 minutes.

Makes about 32 meatballs

Cocktail meatballs taste even better when made a day ahead and reheated.

Corned Beef & Green Onion Cheese Ball

Utensil: 3-qt stainless steel bowl

3   (2½ oz) pkgs corned beef
3   (8 oz) pkgs lite cream cheese
1   bunch green onions; chopped
1   tsp garlic powder
2   tbsp Worcestershire sauce
2   tbsp Accent flavor enhancer

Cut corned beef into small bite-size pieces. Mix all ingredients together in bowl. Mold into 2 balls. Refrigerate 2 hours. Serve with crackers.

Chicken Stuffed Mushrooms

Utensils: Saladmaster Food Processor, 11" skillet, stainless steel cookie sheet, 1-qt sauce pan

2 boneless, skinless chicken breasts
16 medium, fresh mushrooms
1 small onion
2 tbsp margarine
1 slice bread; torn into small pieces
2 tbsp cooking sherry
¼ tsp marjoram
⅛ tsp freshly ground black pepper
⅛ tsp oregano

Remove excess fat from chicken breasts; cut into small, bite-size pieces. Preheat skillet on medium-high. Brown chicken in uncovered skillet; remove and set aside. Preheat oven broiler.

Clean mushrooms with vegetable brush. Remove and finely chop stems; save mushroom caps. Chop onion using #2 Stringer food processor cone. Melt 1 tbsp margarine in skillet at medium-high heat. Saute mushroom stems and onion until tender. Add bread, sherry, marjoram, pepper and oregano to saute.

In sauce pan melt remaining margarine at medium-low heat. Place mushroom caps, round-side up, on cookie sheet; brush with melted margarine. Broil 2 minutes; remove from oven. Invert mushroom caps; fill with chicken-saute mixture. Brush with remaining melted margarine. Broil 3 minutes.

Zesty Chicken Wings

Utensils: Electric skillet,
2-qt and 3-qt stainless steel bowls

- 2 lbs chicken wings
- ½ tsp freshly ground ginger
- ½ tsp minced garlic
- ⅓ cup pineapple juice
- ¼ cup water
- ¼ cup lite soy sauce
- ⅛ tsp cayenne pepper

Cut chicken wings at both joints; save pointy ends for stock. Place wings in 3-qt bowl. Combine remaining ingredients in 2-qt bowl; pour over chicken. Cover; refrigerate 24 hours.

Drain marinade; reserve. Preheat electric skillet at 300°. Add chicken and ¼ cup marinade; cover. When Vapo-Valve "clicks," reduce heat to simmer. Cook 30 minutes.

Serves 8-10

GINGERROOT

Substitute: *Use ¼ teaspoon of ground ginger in place of 1 teaspoon fresh-grated gingerroot.*

Suggestion: *Store in the refrigerator crisper. Do not enclose in plastic. Break off pieces as needed.*

Skillet Toastwiches

Utensils: Electric skillet, Saladmaster Food Processor,
3-qt stainless steel bowl, 9" pie pan

1 cup grated American cheese
1 tbsp chopped onion
1 (12 oz) can corned beef
½ cup chopped pickles
¼ cup mayonnaise
12 slices bread
 Mustard
2 tbsp margarine
2 eggs
¾ cup evaporated milk

Grate cheese using #1 Shredder food processor cone. Chop onion using #2 Stringer cone.

In bowl mix beef, cheese, onion, pickles and mayonnaise. Spread bread lightly with mustard. Spoon beef mixture on 6 slices of bread; top with remaining bread slices. Place margarine in skillet; melt at 350°. Beat eggs lightly in pie pan. Add milk; mix well. Place both sides of sandwich into egg/milk mixture. Lay in skillet; brown each side 2-3 minutes.

Makes 6 sandwiches

Skillet Popcorn

Utensils: Electric skillet, high dome cover

3 tbsp canola oil
½ cup popcorn

Preheat electric skillet at 400°. Add oil and popcorn. Cover with high dome cover; cook until all corn is popped. Turn skillet over to allow popcorn to empty into dome cover. Serve from cover.

Makes 8 cups

Electric Skillet Pizza

Utensils: Electric skillet, Saladmaster Food Processor

2½ cups grated mozzarella cheese
¼ lb Italian sausage
    Prepared pizza dough
5 tbsp pizza sauce
    Pepperoni slices

Grate cheese using #2 Stringer food processor cone.

Preheat skillet at 325°. Add Italian sausage; brown. Remove sausage; set aside. Drain off sausage grease; let skillet cool. Place dough in bottom of skillet; shape to fit pan. Spread pizza sauce over dough. Top sauce with cheese. Add sausage and pepperoni slices. Cover; cook 10 minutes at 325°. Turn unit off; let stand 10-15 minutes. (Note: DO NOT LIFT LID DURING COOKING TIME.)

Serves 4

Prepare pizza dough by using a dry mix which takes from 20 to 30 minutes. You can also purchase prepared pizza dough in the refrigerated section of your grocery, usually with the canned biscuits.

As optional toppings add mushrooms, bell pepper, onion, olives.

Soups/Stews
Salads/Sauces

Creamy Spinach Soup

Utensils: 2-qt sauce pan, Saladmaster Food Processor

½	cup shredded carrots
½	cup chopped onion
2	tbsp margarine
2	tbsp flour
1	tsp salt or seasoning substitute
½	tsp dry mustard
1	(14½ oz) can low-salt chicken broth
1	(10 oz) pkg frozen chopped spinach
2½	cups milk
1	tbsp fresh lemon juice

Shred carrots and chop onion using #1 Shredder food processor cone.

Place margarine in sauce pan; melt at medium-low heat. Blend in flour, salt or seasoning and mustard. Remove from heat; stir in chicken broth. Heat to boil over medium heat; stir constantly. Add spinach, carrots and onion. Cook over medium heat until spinach is thawed and vegetables are tender. Stir in milk and lemon juice. Reduce heat to medium-low; cook 2-3 minutes.

Serves 6

Eating foods with large amounts of sodium has been linked to high blood pressure in some people. It is wise to avoid adding salt at the table or during cooking. Also, be aware of hidden sources for salt. Read ingredient labels for salt in canned, dried, frozen or other processed foods, such as cheeses, pickles and beverages.

Low Cholesterol Chicken and Lime Soup

Utensils: 11" skillet, 6-qt Dutch oven, Saladmaster Food Processor

¼ tsp finely shredded lime peel
½ cup chopped onion
4 boneless, skinless chicken breast halves
2 6" flour tortillas
6 cups chicken broth
1 (4 oz) can diced green chili peppers; drained
½ tsp dried oregano; crushed
2 tbsp lime juice
⅛ tsp black pepper
1 clove garlic; minced
1 cup chopped tomato
2 tbsp snipped parsley or cilantro

Shred lime peel using #1 Shredder food processor cone. Chop onions using #2 Stringer cone.

Cut chicken breasts into bite-size pieces. Cut each tortilla into 5 wedges. Preheat skillet on medium heat. Place tortillas in skillet; toast 8-10 minutes or until light brown. Remove from skillet; cool.

In Dutch oven combine chicken broth, onion, chili peppers, oregano, lime peel, lime juice, black pepper and garlic. Bring to boil. Reduce heat to low; simmer 5 minutes. Stir in chicken; cook 7-9 minutes or until chicken is tender. Stir in tomato; heat thoroughly.

Sprinkle serving with parsley or cilantro. Serve with tortilla wedges.

Serves 5

Low Cholesterol Vegetable/Chicken Noodle Soup

Utensils: 6-qt Dutch oven, Saladmaster Food Processor

1	cup chopped onion
8	cups water
4	boneless, skinless chicken breasts
6	chicken bouillon cubes
1	tsp majoram; crushed
½	tsp black pepper
1	clove garlic; halved
1	(10 oz) package frozen succotash
3	oz medium or wide egg noodles
½	cup chopped green or red bell pepper
¼	cup snipped parsley

Chop onion using #2 Stringer food processor cone.

In Dutch oven combine water, chicken, bouillon cubes, marjoram, black pepper and garlic. Bring to boil; reduce heat to low. Cover; simmer 1 hour until chicken is tender. Remove chicken; cool until easy to handle. Cut chicken into bite-size pieces. Set aside.

Strain broth; return broth to Dutch oven. Skim fat off broth. Add succotash, noodles, onion and bell pepper to broth. Bring to boil. Reduce heat to low; simmer 10 minutes until noodles are done. Stir in parsley and chicken. Heat thoroughly.

Serves 6

ALTERNATIVE:
If you can't find succotash at your grocery store, use 1 cup frozen corn and 1 cup frozen lima beans.

Garden Vegetable Soup

Utensils: Saladmaster Food Processor, 6-qt Dutch oven

3 medium carrots; scraped, sliced
2 medium celery stalks; chopped
1 medium onion; chopped
1 cup shredded cabbage
1 (28 oz) can whole tomatoes; undrained
2 medium potatoes; peeled, cubed
½ cup uncooked rice
7 cups water
5 beef bouillon cubes
½ tsp dried whole sage
½ tsp dried whole rosemary
⅛ tsp dried whole basil

Slice carrots and chop celery using #4 Thin Slicer food processor cone. Chop onion and shred cabbage using #2 Stringer cone.

Combine all ingredients, except cabbage, in Dutch oven; stir well. Cover; bring to boil at medium-high heat. Reduce heat to low; simmer 20 minutes or until vegetables are crisp/tender. Add cabbage; simmer 7 minutes.

Makes 5 quarts

Vegetable Bean Soup with Ham

Utensils: 6-qt Dutch oven, Saladmaster Food Processor

1   cup sliced carrot
1½ cups shredded fresh spinach or cabbage
1   cup chopped onion
½   cup sliced celery
¾   cup dry navy beans
9   cups water
3   chicken bouillon cubes
1   tsp dried basil; crushed
½   tsp dried thyme; crushed
¼   tsp freshly ground black pepper
2   bay leaves
1   clove garlic; minced
1½ cups diced, cooked ham

Slice carrot and shred fresh spinach or cabbage using #1 Shredder food processor cone. Chop onion using #2 Stringer cone. Slice celery using #4 Thin Slicer cone.

Rinse beans. In Dutch oven combine beans and 4 cups of water. Bring to boil over medium heat. Reduce heat to low; simmer 2 minutes. Remove from heat. Cover; let stand 1 hour.

Drain and rinse beans. Return beans to Dutch oven. Add 5 cups water, carrot, onion, celery, bouillon cubes, basil, thyme, pepper, bay leaves and garlic. Bring to boil over medium heat; reduce heat to low. Cover; simmer 1-2 hours or until beans are tender. Stir in ham and spinach or cabbage; simmer 3-5 minutes. Remove bay leaves.

Serves 5

Option: *Soak beans overnight in covered pan.*

Simple Chili

Utensils: 6-qt Dutch oven, Saladmaster Food Processor

OPTION: *Include 1 (16 oz) can kidney beans when adding tomatoes, etc. Cook additional 15 minutes.*

2 lbs chili meat
1 large onion
1 clove garlic; minced
1 tsp salt or seasoning substitute
2 tsp freshly ground black pepper
2 tsp cayenne pepper
4 tbsp chili pepper
½ tsp basil
½ tsp savory
3 bay leaves
1 (14 oz) can tomato sauce
1 (14 oz) can peeled whole tomatoes
1 cup water

Preheat Dutch oven at medium heat. Add chili meat; brown.

Chop onion using #2 Stinger food processor cone. Mix onion and garlic with chili meat in Dutch oven; cook until onions are tender. Add remaining ingredients; cover. When Vapo-Valve "clicks," reduce heat to low. Simmer 1 hour. Remove bay leaves.

Serves 6

Turkey-Vegetable Chili

Utensil: 3-qt sauce pan

½ cup chopped bell pepper
¼ cup chopped small onion
2 cloves garlic; finely chopped
2 tsp olive oil
3 cups diced, cooked turkey or chicken
½ cup water
1 tbsp dried oregano
1 tbsp chili powder
1 tsp ground cumin
1 (16 oz) can whole tomatoes; undrained, crushed
1 (10 oz) pkg frozen mixed vegetables
2 cups ½" sliced zucchini

Pour oil in sauce pan; heat on medium. Add bell pepper, onion and garlic. Saute 3 minutes, stirring frequently, until onion is tender. Stir in remaining ingredients except frozen vegetables and zucchini. Heat to boil over medium heat; reduce heat to low. Cover; simmer 1 hour, stirring occasionally. Stir in frozen vegetables and zucchini. Return to boil over medium heat; reduce heat to low. Simmer uncovered 5 minutes, stirring occasionally, until zucchini is crisp/tender.

Serves 6

Make your own homemade flavorful blend of chili seasoning. Combine 3 tbsp pure ground chili pepper, 1½ tbsp ground cumin, 1 tsp dried oregano, ½ tsp ground cayenne pepper, ½ tsp rubbed sage and ½ tsp ground allspice. Store in a covered jar in cool, dry place. Makes ¼ cup.

Irish Stew

Utensil: 6-qt Dutch oven

2   lbs stewing lamb or beef
¼   cup sliced onion
6   cups hot water
½   cup diced celery
1   cup diced carrots
1   cup cubed turnips
1   cup cubed potato
2   tsp salt substitute
½   tsp black pepper

Cut meat into small pieces. Preheat Dutch oven on medium. Add meat; brown. Add remaining ingredients. Cover; cook on medium heat 3 minutes. Reduce heat to low; cook 3 hours.

Serves 4

Spicy Fruited Beef Stew

Utensil: 6-qt Dutch oven

1	lb beef stew meat; cut into 1″ cubes
4	cups water
1	tbsp vinegar
2	beef bouillon cubes
½	tsp ground cinnamon
⅛	tsp ground cloves
⅛	tsp black pepper
1	(8 oz) pkg mixed dried fruit
1	(16 oz) pkg frozen small whole onions
2	cups 1″ cubed potatoes
1½	cups 1″ bias-sliced carrots

Preheat Dutch oven on medium. Add meat; brown. Add water, vinegar, bouillon cubes, cinnamon, cloves and pepper. Bring to boil; reduce heat to low. Cover; simmer 1 hour.

Cut up large pieces of dried fruit. Add dried fruit, onions, potatoes and carrots to meat mixture. Cover; simmer 30-40 minutes or until meat and vegetables are tender.

Serves 6

Lamb Stew

Utensils: 6-qt Dutch oven, 1-qt stainless steel bowl

1½ lbs lean boneless lamb
1 (14½ oz) can tomatoes; cut, undrained
1 cup water; divided
½ cup dry white wine
2½ cups ½" sliced peeled parsnips
2 cups fresh cut green beans
1 cup ½" sliced carrots
½ cup chopped onion
1 tsp dried rosemary; crushed
⅛ tsp black pepper
1 clove garlic; minced
2 tbsp cornstarch
⅓ cup low-fat plain yogurt

Trim fat from lamb; cut meat into 1" cubes.

In Dutch oven combine lamb, tomatoes, ¾ cup water, wine, parsnips, green beans, carrots, onion, rosemary, pepper and garlic. Cover; cook over medium heat 1¼-1½ hours or until lamb is tender.

Combine cornstarch and ¼ cup water in bowl. Stir into lamb mixture. Cook over medium heat; stirring until thick and bubbly. Cook additional 2 minutes. Dollop yogurt atop each serving.

Serves 6

Crab Gumbo

Utensil: 3-qt sauce pan

1   tbsp canola oil
½   cup chopped bell pepper
½   cup sliced green onion
1   clove garlic; minced
3   cups chicken broth
2   medium tomatoes; peeled, chopped
⅛   tsp celery salt
⅛   tsp dried thyme; crushed
⅛   tsp hot pepper sauce
1   cup frozen sliced okra
1   (6 oz) can crabmeat
½   cup diced turkey ham
2   cups hot cooked rice (page 97)

Pour oil in sauce pan; heat at medium. Add bell pepper, green onion and garlic. Saute until vegetables are tender. Stir in chicken broth, tomatoes, celery salt, thyme and pepper sauce. Bring to boil over medium heat. Stir in okra; reduce heat to low. Cover; simmer 10 minutes or until okra is tender.

Drain, flake and remove cartilage from crabmeat. Stir crabmeat and turkey ham into gumbo. Heat thoroughly on medium. Serve over rice in soup bowl.

Serves 4

To keep unused cloves of garlic fresh, peel the cloves and place them in a small jar filled with olive oil. Cover and refrigerate. The garlic stays fresh and is ready for use. The oil makes a great ingredient in salad dressings.

Fiesta Taco Salad

Utensils: 8" skillet, Saladmaster Food Processor

Optional toppings for Fiesta Taco Salad: black olives, sour cream, guacamole, salsa

1   cup grated Cheddar cheese
1   medium onion
1   lb lean ground beef
1   (1¼ oz) pkg taco sauce mix
¾   cup water
1   (7 oz) pkg nacho cheese tortilla chips; crushed
1   head lettuce
3   tomatoes; chopped

Grate cheese using #1 Shredder food processor cone. Chop onion using #2 Stringer cone.

Preheat skillet on medium. Add meat; brown and drain. Add onion, taco sauce mix and water. Reduce heat to low; simmer 5 minutes. Refrigerate until cool.

Crush tortilla chips. Add lettuce, tomatoes, cheese, tortilla chips to meat; toss together.

Serves 6-8

Health Salad

Utensils: Saladmaster Food Processor,
3-qt stainless steel bowl

½ cup grated Cheddar cheese
1 medium carrot
⅓ head green cabbage
¼ head red cabbage
3 radishes
½ cucumber

Grate cheese, cut carrot and shred cabbages using #1 Shredder food processor cone. Slice radishes and cucumber using #4 Thin Slicer cone.

Toss all ingredients in bowl. Serve with lite salad dressing.

Serves 6 to 8

Note: *For easy cleaning of #1 Shredder food processor cone, cut carrot after cheese.*

Fresh Spinach Salad with Apple

Utensils: 1-qt sauce pan, Saladmaster Food Processor, 3-qt stainless steel bowl

1 lb fresh spinach
1 cup chopped apple
½ cup chopped celery
1 tbsp lemon juice
¼ cup balsamic vinegar
¼ cup olive oil
2 tsp honey
1 tsp caraway seeds

Wash, dry and remove stems from spinach; tear into bite-size pieces.

Chop apple using #3 French Fryer food processor cone. Chop celery using #4 Thin Slicer cone.

Combine spinach, apples and celery in bowl. Sprinkle with lemon juice; toss well.

Combine vinegar, oil, honey and caraway seeds in sauce pan. Bring to boil over medium heat. Pour liquid over spinach mixture; toss well. Serve immediately.

Serves 10

Saladmaster Fruit Salad

Utensils: Saladmaster Food Processor,
3-qt stainless steel bowl

3 large apples
4 bananas
1 lemon
1 orange
1 cup pecans
1 (8 oz) can crushed pineapple; undrained

Cut apples using #3 French Fryer food processor cone. Cut bananas using #5 Waffler cone. Grate lemon and orange rinds and chop pecans using #1 Shredder cone.

Place apples and bananas in bowl. Pour pineapple over fruit to keep air from discoloring; stir. Slice lemon and orange. Add pecans, lemon and orange slices. Top with orange and lemon rind.

Serves 6-8

These are the top ten fibrous foods:

- *Raw green bell peppers*
- *Black-eyed peas*
- *Blueberries*
- *Bran cereal*
- *Lima beans*
- *Blackberries*
- *Green peas*
- *Wheat cereal*
- *Pinto beans*
- *Oats*

Black-Eyed Pea Salad

Utensils: 3-qt sauce pan, Saladmaster Food Processor,
2-qt stainless steel bowl

10 cups water
2 cups dry black-eyed peas
¼ cup chopped onion
½ cup chopped bell pepper
2 tbsp finely chopped canned jalapeno peppers
2 tbsp canola or olive oil
2 tbsp red wine vinegar
1 clove garlic; minced
¼ tsp freshly ground black pepper

Pour 6 cups water in sauce pan. Add peas; soak overnight. Drain off water. Add 4 cups water; cook over low heat 1½ hours. Rinse in cold water; drain.

Cut onion using #2 Stringer food processor cone.

In bowl combine onion and all remaining ingredients; mix well. Add to peas; chill 1 hour.

Serves 6

Summer Pasta Salad

Utensils: 2-qt sauce pan, 2-qt and 3-qt stainless steel bowls

3	cups cooked pasta spirals
¾	cup low-fat plain yogurt
¼	cup cider vinegar
2	tbsp grated Parmesan cheese
2	tbsp lite mayonnaise
½	tsp garlic powder
½	tsp freshly ground black pepper
1½	cups broccoli florets
½	cup sliced carrots
1½	cups sliced zucchini

Cook pasta according to pkg directions in sauce pan; omit salt. Drain; rinse under cold water. Set aside.

In 2-qt bowl mix yogurt, vinegar, Parmesan cheese, mayonnaise, garlic powder and pepper. Set aside.

In 3-qt bowl combine pasta, yogurt mixture and vegetables; mix well. Chill thoroughly; serve cold.

Serves 4

Marinated Cucumber Salad

Utensils: Saladmaster Food Processor, 2-qt and 3-qt stainless steel bowls

2½	cups sliced cucumber
¼	tsp salt substitute
⅓	cup vinegar
3	tbsp sugar
1	tbsp water

Slice cucumber using #5 Waffler food processor cone.

Place cucumber slices in 3-qt bowl; sprinkle with salt substitute. In 2-qt bowl combine vinegar, sugar and water; stir until sugar dissolves. Pour over cucumber slices; toss lightly to coat. Cover; chill 30 minutes. Serve with slotted spoon.

Serves 4

Waldorf Salad

*Utensils: Saladmaster Food Processor,
2-qt and 3-qt stainless steel bowls*

1 medium golden apple
1 medium red apple
2 cups chopped celery
½ cup raisins
½ cup warm water
½ cup plain low-fat plain yogurt
¼ cup lite mayonnaise
¼ cup nonfat buttermilk
1 cup seedless green grapes; halved

Cut unpeeled apples and chop celery using #2
Stringer food processor cone.

In 2-qt bowl combine raisins and warm water; set
aside 30 minutes to plump raisins. Combine yogurt,
mayonnaise and buttermilk in container of an electric
blender; process until smooth. Transfer yogurt
mixture to 3-qt bowl. Drain raisins; add to yogurt
mixture. Add apples, celery and grapes. Toss lightly;
coat well. Cover; chill 1 hour.

Serves 8

Coleslaw with Fruit

Utensils: Saladmaster Food Processor,
3-qt stainless steel bowl

- 1   medium carrot
- 3   medium apples
- ⅓   head cabbage
- 1   (16 oz) can pineapple tidbits

Cut carrot using #1 Shredder food processor cone.
Cut apples and cabbage using #2 Stringer cone.

Toss all ingredients together in bowl. Before serving,
mix with coleslaw dressing (below).

COLESLAW DRESSING NO. 1

- ¼   cup vinegar
- ½   cup sugar
- 1   cup lite mayonnaise or salad dressing

Place all ingredients in container; shake well.

COLESLAW DRESSING NO. 2

- 2   tbsp lite mayonnaise
- 4   tbsp honey
- 6   tbsp cider vinegar

Place ingredients in container; shake vigorously.

COLESLAW DRESSING

Utensil: 2-qt stainless steel bowl

- ⅓   cup sugar
- ⅓   cup vinegar
- 1   cup lite salad dressing

Place all ingredients in bowl; stir until smooth.

Honey is healthier for you than sugar. But a tablespoon of honey has 65 calories, compared to 45 calories in a tablespoon of white sugar and 50 calories in a tablespoon of brown sugar.

Buttermilk Salad Dressing

Utensil: 3-qt stainless steel bowl

1   cup buttermilk
½   cup lite mayonnaise
¼   cup low-fat plain yogurt
2   tbsp chopped parsley
1   tbsp chopped chives
1   tsp sugar
½   tsp dried oregano; crushed
½   tsp dried basil; crushed
¼   tsp dried marjoram; crushed
⅛   tsp black pepper

In bowl mix all ingredients together. Chill 1 hour.

Makes 1¾ cups

Horseradish Dressing

Utensil: 3-qt stainless steel bowl

½   cup lite mayonnaise or salad dressing
½   cup low-fat plain yogurt
2½ tbsp chives; snipped
1½ tbsp prepared horseradish
1   tsp poppy seeds
¾   cup skim milk

In bowl mix mayonnaise, yogurt, chives, horseradish and poppy seeds. Slowly blend in milk. Cover; chill 1 hour.

Makes 1½ cups

Sweet and Sour Sauce

Utensil: 1-qt sauce pan

½ cup honey
1½ tbsp cornstarch
1 tbsp lite soy sauce
¼ tsp freshly ground black pepper
½ cup red wine vinegar
½ cup pineapple juice
¼ tsp ground ginger
¼ tsp garlic powder
¼ tsp chives

In sauce pan mix honey with cornstarch. Add all remaining ingredients. Bring to boil over medium heat; stir continually until thick. Reduce heat to low; simmer 1 minute. Serve warm or add to stir-fry recipes.

Makes 1¼ cups

This is a standard wok cooking sauce which can be used in place of oil to provide both added flavor and better health.

Cornstarch Low Calorie Gravy

Utensil: 1-qt sauce pan

   Meat Broth
¼ cup water
   Cornstarch

After roasting any main dish meat, remove meat from utensil and pour remaining liquid broth into sauce pan.

Add water to liquid. Bring to boil over medium heat. Season to taste. Add cornstarch to boiling broth; thicken to desired consistency.

For chicken gravy, substitute milk for water.

Main Dishes

Vegetarian Wok

Utensil: Wok

1   tsp olive oil
1   whole garlic clove
1   zucchini; cut into long strips
1   yellow squash
1   cup broccoli tops
2   carrots; cut into long thin strips
1   bell pepper; sliced
1   onion; sliced
1   tsp grated fresh ginger root
1   (8 oz) can sliced water chestnuts
¼   cup lite soy sauce
1   (8 oz) can pineapple chunks
1   (6 oz) can mandarin oranges

Pour oil into wok; preheat on medium-high. Add garlic clove; sear and remove. Combine vegetables in wok; stir together 5 minutes. Add ginger root, water chestnuts, soy sauce and fruit. Cover; cook 2 minutes. Remove from heat; let set 5 minutes.

Serves 4

Because of the unique 5-ply construction of the Saladmaster Wok, you can stir-fry most vegetables and meats without the use of oil.

Here are some additional tips to increase your cooking enjoyment:
- *Partially freeze meat to make it easier to slice.*
- *Dust meats with cornstarch before cooking to prevent loss of meat juices.*
- *Meats can be marinated hours or days before cooking. Refrigerate in sealed, air-tight container.*
- *Add sauce after fish or meat is partially cooked. When added too early, sauce may cause toughening of meat.*
- *Before adding food, always preheat wok over medium-high until 1-2 drops of water skitter when sprinkled in the wok.*

Stuffed Tomatoes

Utensils: 2-qt sauce pan, 3-qt stainless steel bowl

1 cup 4-color corkscrew macaroni
1 (7½ oz) can salmon; drained, flaked,
   skin and bones removed
½ cup low-fat plain yogurt
½ cup grated cucumber
¼ cup grated carrot
2 tbsp lite mayonnaise
¼ tsp dried dillweed
4 medium tomatoes

Cook macaroni according to package directions in sauce pan. Drain; set aside.

In bowl combine salmon, yogurt, cucumber, carrot, mayonnaise and dillweed. Add pasta; toss. Cover; chill 4 hours.

Cut out ½″ core from each tomato. Invert tomatoes. For each, make cut from top to, but not quite through, the stem end forming 6 wedges.

To serve, place tomatoes on plates. Spread wedges slightly apart. Fill with salmon-pasta mixture.

Serves 4

While fish is generally considered a low-fat protein source, fat content does vary. Here is the percentage of fat content in a variety of fish:
- *Very low in fat (less than 2%) - cod, halibut, rockfish, sea bass*
- *Low in fat (2%-5%) - bluefish, catfish, flounder, haddock, red snapper, shark, sole, turbot*
- *Moderately high in fat (6%-10%) - albacore tuna, mullet, pompano, salmon, swordfish, trout*
- *Relatively high in fat (more than 10%) - mackerel, shad, shad roe*

Saladmaster Roast

Utensil: 6-qt Dutch oven

4	lb pot roast
½	tsp garlic powder
1	tsp freshly ground black pepper
2	tsp salt substitute
5	carrots; cut in 3″ lengths
5	potatoes; halved
1	large yellow onion; quartered

Preheat Dutch oven over medium heat. Place roast in Dutch oven; sear 10 minutes or until meat loosens in pan. Turn roast; season with garlic powder, pepper and salt substitute. Sear 10 minutes. Add vegetables; reduce heat to low. Cover; cook 1½ hours or until tender.

GRAVY

Utensil: 1-qt stainless steel bowl

1	can lite beef broth
1½	tbsp cornstarch

Pour broth into bowl; stir in cornstarch. Pour over roast. Simmer until thick.

TIME CHART
*For Range Top
Roasting*

*Beef, rare
   10 minutes per lb
Beef, medium
   15 minutes per lb
Beef, well done
   20 minutes per lb
Ham, fresh
   25 minutes per lb
Lamb, leg
   20 minutes per lb
Pork
   20 minutes per lb
Poultry
   15 minutes per lb
Veal
   20 minutes per lb*

Fruited Pot Roast

Utensils: 6-qt Dutch oven, 2-qt sauce pan

4	lb pot roast
¾	cup apple juice
¾	cup water
2	3″ cinnamon sticks
1	(6 oz) pkg dried apricots
1	cup pitted prunes
1	large cooking apple; peeled, sliced

Preheat Dutch oven over medium heat. Place roast in Dutch oven; sear 10 minutes or until meat loosens in pan. Turn roast; sear 10 minutes.

In sauce pan mix apple juice and water; add cinnamon sticks. Cover; cook over medium heat until Vapo-Valve "clicks." Reduce heat to low; cook 1 hour. Add apricots, prunes and apple. Cover; simmer 30 minutes. Add fruit/sauce to meat. Cover; cook 1½ hours or until tender.

Serves 6

Ship Wreck

Utensils: 11″ skillet, Saladmaster Food Processor

1	onion
4	potatoes
2	lbs ground beef
½	cup uncooked rice
1	(15 oz) can kidney beans; slightly drained
1	(8 oz) can tomato sauce

Chop onion using #2 Stringer food processor cone. Slice potatoes using #4 Thin Slicer cone.

Pat beef into bottom of skillet. Spoon onion onto beef. Arrange potatoes on top of onion. Sprinkle rice around outer edge of skillet. Spoon beans onto rice and potatoes. Pour tomato sauce on top of beans. Cover; cook over medium heat until Vapo-Valve "clicks." Reduce heat to low; cook 35-40 minutes.

Serves 6

Cutting down on excess fats is the most important aspect of cooking meat. Buy lean cuts and trim off visible fat.

Another way to reduce fat is through degreasing. When meat is cooked, pour off melted fats before proceeding with your recipe.

When meats and meat dishes are refrigerated, fat solidifies. This will help to preserve stocks and meat liquids, but should be lifted off and discarded before reheating the dishes.

Pan Broiled Steak

Utensil: 11" skillet

4   boneless ribeye steaks; 1" thick

Preheat skillet on medium heat. Place steak in hot skillet; cook until meat is brown. Turn; brown other side. Continue cooking to desired degree of doneness. Season to taste.

Serves 4

Oriental Pepper Steak

Utensils: Wok, Saladmaster Food Processor

1   onion; chopped fine
1½ lbs lean round steak; cut into thin strips
2   tbsp Worcestershire sauce
2   tbsp lite soy sauce
1½ cups water
3   bell peppers; cut into strips
1   tbsp Wondra flour
1   (16 oz) can whole tomatoes; peeled,
       cut in chunks

Chop onion using #1 Shredder food processor cone.

Preheat wok on medium-high; add onion and meat. Saute until meat is slightly brown. Reduce heat to medium. Add Worcestershire sauce, soy sauce and water; cook 20 minutes.

Add bell pepper; cook 10 minutes. Add flour to make a thin sauce. Add tomatoes; cook 10 minutes.

Serve over cooked whole grain rice.

Serves 6

Note: *If skillet is preheated, steak will stick but will come loose from pan as it cooks.*

COOKING TIME
Pan Broiled Steak

RARE
   4 min. one side
   3 min. other side
MEDIUM RARE
   5 min. one side
   4 min. other side
MEDIUM
   6 min. one side
   5 min. other side
WELL DONE
   7 min. one side
   6 min. other side

Zucchini & Beef Parmesan

Utensils: Electric skillet, Saladmaster Food Processor

2   onions
½   cup grated lite Cheddar cheese
4   zucchini
1   lb lean ground beef
1   (16 oz) can chopped tomatoes; drained
1   (8 oz) can tomato sauce
1   (6 oz) can tomato paste
1   medium bell pepper; chopped
½   tsp dried whole oregano
¼   tsp garlic powder
¼   tsp black pepper
¼   cup grated Parmesan cheese

Cut onions and grate Cheddar cheese using #2 Stringer food processor cone. Cut zucchini using #3 French Fryer cone.

Combine meat and onion in electric skillet. Cover; cook at 325°, stirring occasionally until meat is browned and onion is tender.

Add tomatoes, tomato sauce, tomato paste and bell pepper. Cover; cook at 325° until Vapo-Valve "clicks." Reduce heat to low.

Stir in Cheddar cheese, oregano, garlic powder and black pepper. Add zucchini. Cover; simmer 10 minutes. Sprinkle with Parmesan cheese. Cover; simmer 10 minutes.

Serves 6-8

Burgundy Beef

*Utensils: Electric skillet, Saladmaster Food Processor,
3-qt stainless steel bowl*

1 clove garlic
1 onion
1 lb lean boneless sirloin steak
1 tbsp canola oil
½ lb fresh mushrooms; sliced
¼ cup flour
½ tsp salt
⅛ tsp thyme
⅛ tsp marjoram
⅛ tsp black pepper
¼ tsp garlic powder
2 cups low-fat beef broth
2 cups Burgundy or dry red wine
2 cups hot cooked noodles

Mince clove garlic using #1 Shredder food processor cone. Cut onion using #2 Stringer cone.

Trim fat from steak; cut into 2″ x ¾″ strips. Pour oil in skillet; heat at 325°. Add meat; cook until browned. Turn; cook until evenly browned. Add onion and garlic; cook until onions are transparent, stirring frequently. Add mushrooms; cook 1 minute, stirring frequently.

In bowl combine flour and seasonings; stir until well blended. Add broth and wine; mix well. Pour mixture over meat; stir well.

Cover; cook at 325° until Vapo-Valve "clicks." Reduce temperature to 225°; simmer 35-40 minutes or until meat is tender. Serve over bed of noodles.

Serves 4-6

You can use the following chart for selecting meats:

- *1 oz of ground beef – 81 calories*
- *1 oz of lean sirloin steak – 58 calories*
- *1 oz of lean T-bone steak – 63 calories*
- *1 oz of chicken breast with skin – 56 calories*
- *1 oz of steamed halibut – 37 calories*
- *1 oz of canned salmon – 43 calories*
- *1 oz of boiled shrimp – 33 calories*
- *1 oz of tuna, canned in water – 36 calories*
- *1 link sausage – 48 calories*
- *1 hot dog – 183 calories*

Mexican Corn Casserole

Utensils: Electric skillet, 2-qt sauce pan, Saladmaster Food Processor

1   medium onion
1   cup grated lite Cheddar cheese
1   cup chopped celery
1   cup rice (page 97)
1   lb lean ground beef
1   medium bell pepper; chopped
1   large jalapeno; sliced
2   (17 oz) cans cream-style corn

Cut onion, grate cheese and chop celery using #2 Stringer food processor cone.

Cook rice; set aside. Preheat electric skillet at 375°. Add beef, onion, celery and bell pepper. Saute 15 minutes stirring occasionally; add rice. Add jalapeno slices, corn and cheese; stir well. Reduce heat to low. Cover; simmer 40-45 minutes. Remove cover; let stand 10 minutes before serving.

Serves 8-10

All-In-One Meal

Utensils: 11" skillet, Saladmaster Food Processor

1   large potato
¼   head cabbage
2   carrots
1   medium onion
1   lb lean ground beef
1   (10¾ oz) can cream of chicken soup
8   slices lite Cheddar cheese

Cut potato, cabbage, carrots and onion using #2 Stringer food processor cone. Pat ¾ lb ground beef in bottom of skillet. Add vegetables in layers. Crumble remainder of ground beef on top of vegetables. Spread on soup; place slices of cheese on top. Cover; cook at medium heat until Vapo-Valve "clicks." Reduce heat to low; cook 20 minutes.

Serves 4

Skillet Meatloaf

- 1 small onion
- 1 medium potato
- 1 (8 oz) can tomato sauce; divided
- 2 lbs ground beef
- 2 eggs; slightly beaten
- 1 tsp salt substitute
- ½ cup grated Cheddar cheese

Chop onion using #2 Stringer food processor cone. Grate potato using #1 Shredder cone.

Measure ⅓ cup tomato sauce; set aside. In bowl mix together onion, potato, beef, remaining tomato sauce, eggs and salt substitute. Mix well; shape into loaf.

Place meat loaf in skillet; top with reserved tomato sauce. Cover; cook over medium heat until Vapo-Valve "clicks." Reduce heat to low; cook 30-35 minutes. Spoon cheese onto meatloaf. Cover; cook 3-4 minutes until cheese melts.

Serves 8

Low-Cal Meatloaf

- 1 lb ground beef
- 2 eggs
- ¼ cup wheat germ
- ¼ cup skim milk
- ½ cup chopped onion
- ⅛ tsp dried sage

Mix all ingredients in bowl. Blend together; shape into loaf.

Place loaf in skillet. Cover; cook at medium heat until Vapo-Valve "clicks." Reduce heat to low; cook 15-20 minutes.

Serves 8

Electric Skillet Lasagna

Utensils: Electric skillet, Saladmaster Food Processor, 3-qt sauce pan, steamer inset, 3-qt stainless steel bowl

6	cups grated mozzarella cheese
4	cups water
2	lbs lean ground beef
1	tsp garlic powder
1	tsp celery salt
1	(1 oz) pkg Italian dry seasoning
1	(6 oz) can tomato paste
1	(16 oz) can tomato sauce
2	(8 oz) ctns low-fat cottage cheese
1	(8 oz) box uncooked lasagna noodles

Grate mozzarella cheese using #2 Stringer food processor cone.

Pour water into sauce pan; bring to boil over medium heat. Place ground beef in steamer; insert into sauce pan. Cover; steam 6 minutes.

In bowl add beef, garlic powder, celery salt, Italian seasoning, tomato paste and tomato sauce; mix well.

In cold electric skillet layer in the following order:

Cover bottom of skillet with ½ meat sauce mixture.
½ of the uncooked lasagna noodles.
Layer of cottage cheese.
Layer of mozzarella.
Layer of remaining meat sauce.
Remaining lasagna noodles.
Cottage cheese.
Mozzarella.

Cover; cook 40 minutes at 275°.

Serves 8-10

Hamburgers

Utensils: 11" skillet, 3-qt stainless steel bowl, 11" utility rack

1   lb ground beef
½   cup chopped onion
4   hambuger buns

In bowl mix ground beef and onion. Shape into
4 patties. Place patties in cold skillet. Cook over
medium heat until brown on both sides. Place utility
rack into skillet. Put buns on rack. Cover; cook 2
minutes.

Serves 4

Oriental Pepper Burgers

Utensils: 11" skillet, 3-qt stainless steel bowl

1   lb ground beef
1   tsp Lowry's seasoning salt
1   tsp freshly ground black pepper
1   tsp onion powder
1   tsp garlic powder
1   medium red onion; chopped
1   green bell pepper; chopped
1   red bell pepper; chopped
1   (8 oz) can tomato sauce
¼   tsp ground ginger
1½ tbsp lite soy sauce

In bowl combine ground beef, seasoning salt, black
pepper, onion powder and garlic powder. Add onion,
green bell pepper and red bell pepper; mix well.
Blend in tomato sauce, ginger and soy sauce. Shape
into 4 patties. Place in skillet. Cover; cook over
medium heat 4 minutes each side.

Serves 4

Swedish Meatballs

*Utensils: 11" skillet, 3-qt stainless steel bowl,
Saladmaster Food Processor*

1   cup chopped onions
3   tbsp margarine
3   slices bread
½   cup milk
2   eggs
1½ lbs lean ground beef
1   tbsp salt substitute
½   tsp freshly ground black pepper
1   tbsp flour
2   beef bouillon cubes
1   cup boiling water
2   tbsp cooking sherry

Chop onion using #2 Stringer food processor cone.

Place margarine in skillet; melt over medium heat.
Add onions; saute until transparent. Remove onions
from skillet; reserve drippings.

In bowl soak bread in milk. Add onions, eggs, ground
beef, salt substitute and pepper to bread mixture; mix
until thoroughly blended. Form into 1½" balls.

Place meatballs in skillet; brown over medium heat.
Remove meatballs from skillet. Add reserved
drippings to skillet. Stir in flour until blended. Add
bouillon and water; stir until sauce is smooth and
thick.

Add meatballs and sherry. Cover; cook over medium
heat until Vapo-Valve "clicks." Reduce heat to low;
simmer 15 minutes.

Makes 40 meatballs

Veal Scallopini

Utensils: Electric skillet, Saladmaster Food Processor

1½ lbs veal cutlets
¼ cup flour
¼ cup margarine
½ lb mushrooms; thinly sliced
1 clove garlic; minced
2 tbsp parsley
2 tbsp basil
½ cup fresh tomatoes; peeled, seeded, diced
½ cup Marsala wine

Rinse veal; pat dry with paper towel. Slash edges of meat in a number of places to keep it from curling up. Coat with flour.

Place margarine in skillet; melt at 325°. Add veal cutlets; cook 5 minutes on both sides. Reduce heat to 200°; add mushrooms and garlic. Cook 1 minute. Add parsley, basil, tomatoes and wine. Cover; simmer 8 minutes. Remove veal; serve with sauce.

Serves 6-8

Sweet and Sour Ribs

Utensil: 11" skillet

3 lbs baby back ribs
1 cup pineapple preserves
½ cup canned whole berry cranberry sauce
½ cup chili sauce
⅓ cup white vinegar
½ cup water

Preheat skillet on medium. Place ribs in skillet; brown on both sides. Add remaining ingredients; mix well.

Cover; bring to boil. When Vapo-Valve "clicks," reduce heat to low. Cook 2 hours or until ribs are tender.

Serves 4

Barbecued Ribs

Utensil: 11" skillet

3 lbs beef short ribs
1 (18 oz) jar barbecue sauce

Preheat skillet at medium-high heat. Add ribs; brown on all sides. Add barbecue sauce.

Cover; reduce heat to medium. When Vapo-Valve "clicks," reduce heat to low. Turn ribs; cook 2 hours or until ribs are tender.

Serves 4

Ways With Ham

Utensil: 11" skillet

2   slices (2 lbs) center cut ham; pre-cooked
1   (12 oz) can Coke or 7-Up

In skillet place ham slices. Pour Coke or 7-Up over ham. Cover; cook on medium heat until Vapo-Valve "clicks." Reduce heat to low; simmer 1 hour.

Serves 4-6

Royal Raisin Sauce

Utensils: 2-qt sauce pan, 1-qt stainless steel bowl

2   cups + 2 tbsp water
1   cup raisins
2   tbsp cornstarch
2   tbsp sugar
1   tbsp margarine
2   tbsp lemon juice

Pour 2 cups water into sauce pan; bring to boil over medium heat. Add raisins to water. Cover; reduce heat to low. Simmer 15 minutes.

In bowl make a paste of cornstarch, sugar and 2 tbsp water. Add to raisins. Heat at medium until thick; stir continually. Remove from heat. Add margarine and lemon juice; mix well. Serve over ham.

Makes 3 cups

Always refrigerate meats while they are marinating. Allowing them to marinate at room temperature encourages bacteria growth.

When refrigerating stuffing or gravies, place them in separate containers, not with the meat, to prevent bacteria growth. Cooked meat and meat dishes should be covered and refrigerated no more than 4 days.

Mexican Pork Chops and Beans

Utensils: Electric skillet, 3-qt stainless steel bowl

2 tbsp flour
1 cup thick chunky salsa
2 tbsp lime juice
¾ tbsp chili powder
½ tsp garlic powder
4 pork chops; ½" thick
1 (16 oz) can light red kidney beans; drained
2 medium red bell peppers; sliced

Preheat electric skillet at 350°.

In bowl mix flour, salsa, lime juice, chili powder and garlic powder; blend well. Place pork chops in skillet; cover with flour mixture.

Spoon beans and pepper slices around pork chops. Cover; cook until Vapo-Valve "clicks." Reduce heat to 225°; simmer 30-40 minutes. Turn control off; let stand 5 minutes.

Serves 4

Although most people don't realize it, beans are just as effective as oat bran in lowering cholesterol. Kidney beans happen to be the American favorite. But you should also add variety to your meals by trying black beans, white beans, lima beans, pinto beans, chowder beans and aduki beans.

Applesauce Pork Chops

Utensil: Electric skillet

6 pork chops
1½ cups applesauce
   Cornstarch

Preheat electric skillet at 375°. Add pork chops; brown both sides. Place ¼ cup applesauce on each pork chop. Cover; cook 20 minutes. Remove pork chops. Slowly stir in cornstarch to thicken remaining meat juice; serve over chops.

Serves 4-6

Pork Chops and Cabbage

Utensils: Electric skillet, Saladmaster Food Processor

⅓ head cabbage
1 medium potato
6 pork chops
1 (10¾ oz) can tomato soup

Cut cabbage using #4 Thin Slicer food processor cone. Cut potato using #5 Waffler cone.

Preheat electric skillet at 375°. Add pork chops; brown both sides. Place potatoes on chops, cabbage on potatoes, and tomato soup on cabbage. Pat down; cook 25 minutes.

Serves 6

NOTE: *For added taste, you can rub meat tenderizer on chops before browning. For a roast, rub some on in the morning and let roast set all night, cooking the next day.*

Bacon

Utensil: 8″ skillet

½ lb bacon strips

Lay bacon strips in cold skillet. Cook on medium heat until grease starts popping. Reduce heat to low; cook until crisp.

Serves 2-4

You can substitute turkey bacon.

Steamed Sausage

Utensils: 3-qt sauce pan, steamer inset

4 cups water
½ lb link sausage

Pour water into sauce pan; bring to boil over medium heat. Place sausage into steamer; insert into sauce pan. Cover; steam 15-20 minutes.

Serves 2-4

Liver Deluxe

Utensils: 11" skillet, Saladmaster Food Processor,
1-qt and 2-qt stainless steel bowls

1   onion
1   cup flour
1   tsp salt substitute
1   tsp freshly ground black pepper
1   lb baby beef liver; sliced
¼   cup margarine
1   (4 oz) can mushrooms; undrained
¼   tsp garlic salt

Cut onion using #2 Stringer food processor cone.

Mix flour, salt substitute and pepper in 2-qt bowl.
Melt margarine in skillet over medium heat. Dredge
pieces of liver in flour mixture. Place liver in skillet;
brown on both sides.

In 1-qt bowl blend onion, mushrooms and garlic salt.
Pour mixture over liver. Cover; cook 25 minutes on
low heat. Remove liver slices to serving platter; top
with onion sauce.

Serves 3-4

These are the
top sources for
Vitamin D:

- *Milk*
- *Eggs*
- *Salmon, sardines,*
  shrimp and tuna
- *Liver*

Smothered Turkey

Utensils: 11" skillet, Saladmaster Food Processor, 2-qt stainless steel bowl

1	medium onion
3	cups hot cooked noodles
2	tbsp snipped fresh parsley
12	oz turkey breast; sliced ¼" thick
2	tsp paprika
1	tsp instant chicken bouillon
¾	cup water
⅛	tsp freshly ground black pepper
⅔	cup low-fat plain yogurt
2	tbsp flour
1	tbsp tomato paste

Slice onion using #4 Thin Slicer food processor cone.

Cook noodles according to package directions. Mix parsley into hot cooked noodles.

Preheat skillet over medium heat. Add turkey slices. Cover; cook 3 minutes each side. Remove turkey slices from skillet; keep warm.

Place onion in skillet. Cook over medium heat until tender. Stir in paprika, bouillon, water and pepper. In bowl combine yogurt, flour and tomato paste. Stir yogurt mixture into skillet. Cook over medium heat; stir until thick and bubbly.

Arrange noodles on a large serving platter; top with turkey slices. Spoon sauce over turkey.

Serves 2-4

Three ounces of turkey without skin has 135 calories but only 55mg of sodium. However, one-half cup of turkey gravy has 60 calories and 235mg of sodium.

Hawaiian Turkey

Utensils: Wok, 2-qt stainless steel bowl

1 tbsp salt
3 tsp oregano
6 cloves garlic
1 tbsp ginger
1 cup olive oil
1 cup vinegar
1 10-12 lb turkey
1 cup brandy
1 (8 oz) can crushed pineapple; undrained
1 (8 oz) jar maraschino cherries; drained
1 fresh orange; peeled, sliced
2 cups dried prunes
1 cup packed brown sugar
1 tsp cloves
  Cornstarch

SUBSTITUTE:
Replace brown sugar with 2 cups honey.

Turkey should be seasoned a day before cooking. In bowl mix salt, oregano, garlic, ginger, olive oil and vinegar. With your hands, spread mixture directly under the skin and inside the cavity of the turkey; refrigerate.

Preheat wok on medium-high heat. Place turkey in wok; brown on all sides. Position turkey in wok with breast down. In bowl mix remaining ingredients; spread over turkey. Cover; cook 1½-2 hours.

Remove turkey from wok; add cornstarch to juices and thicken for gravy.

Serves 10

Turkey Continental

Utensils: 11" skillet, steamer inset, 3-qt sauce pan,
2-qt stainless steel bowl

4	cups water
2	(10 oz) pkgs frozen broccoli spears
8	slices turkey breast
1	(10 oz) can cream of chicken soup
1	cup sour cream
1	(7 oz) jar chopped pimientos
¾	cup grated Swiss cheese

Pour water into sauce pan; bring to boil over medium heat. Place broccoli in steamer; insert into sauce pan. Cover; steam 6 minutes.

Arrange broccoli in skillet. Top with turkey slices. In bowl blend soup and sour cream; pour over top of turkey. Add pimientos; top with cheese. Cover; cook on medium heat until Vapo-Valve "clicks." Reduce heat to low; simmer 25 minutes.

Serves 6

Choose poultry over beef or pork. It has fewer calories, yet is high in protein and B vitamins. To further reduce calories and saturated fat, remove skin before cooking.

Turkey with Mushrooms

Utensils: 11" skillet, Saladmaster Food Processor

1   clove garlic
3   cups fresh mushrooms
1   tbsp margarine
1   lb boneless turkey breast slices; ½" thick
½   cup dry red wine
1   tbsp tomato paste
2   tbsp chopped green onions

Grate garlic using #1 Shredder food processor cone.
Cut mushrooms using #4 Thin Slicer cone.

Place margarine and garlic in skillet; heat at medium.
Place turkey slices in skillet. Cook uncovered 8-10
minutes, turning once, until no longer pink. Remove
turkey; keep warm.

Mix wine and tomato paste in skillet. Stir in
mushrooms. Cook uncovered 3-5 minutes, stirring
occasionally, until mushrooms are tender. Serve
mushrooms over turkey. Sprinkle with onions.

Serves 4

NOTE: *If turkey
pieces are too
thick, flatten each
to ¼"-½" thickness
between sheets of
waxed paper.*

Honey Barbeque Chicken

Utensils: Electric skillet, 3-qt stainless steel bowl

6 boneless, skinless chicken breasts
⅓ cup vinegar
¼ cup honey
2 cloves garlic; minced
2 tsp salt substitute
½ tsp dry mustard
⅛ freshly ground black pepper

Trim fat from chicken; rinse and pat dry with paper towel.

Preheat electric skillet at 375°. Place chicken in skillet; cover with paper towel. Cook 6-7 minutes or until chicken turns loose from bottom of skillet. Turn chicken; brown 6-7 minutes.

In bowl add vinegar, honey, garlic, salt substitute, mustard and pepper; mix well. Pour sauce over chicken. Cover; cook at 375° until Vapo-Valve "clicks." Reduce heat to 200°; simmer 15 minutes.

Serves 4-6

To reduce your salt intake, experts recommend:

• Cutting back gradually. You'll become accustomed to less salt over time.
• Trying the lower-sodium versions of canned soups, salad dressings, sauces and other processed foods.
• Reading labels carefully. According to FDA regulations, "reduced sodium" means a food has 75 percent less sodium than the food it replaces; "low sodium" means it has at most 140mg of sodium per serving; "very low sodium" means no more than 35mg per serving; and "sodium-free" means less than 5mg per serving.
• Adding just a little salt when cooking. Salt gives a sharper taste when it's **on** rather than **in** food.
• Experimenting with herbs and spices, such as bay leaves, oregano, thyme.

Italian Chicken with Spinach

*Utensils: Electric skillet, 1-qt sauce pan,
1-qt stainless steel bowl*

- ⅓ cup grated Parmesan cheese
- ¼ tsp dried Italian seasoning
- 6 boneless, skinless chicken breast halves
- 1 tbsp margarine
- ¼ cup sliced green onion
- 1 tbsp flour
- ½ cup skim milk
- 5 oz frozen chopped spinach; thawed, well drained
- 1 tbsp diced pimiento

In bowl combine Parmesan cheese and Italian seasoning. Roll chicken in cheese mixture; coat lightly. Set remaining cheese mixture aside. Arrange coated chicken breast halves in electric skillet.

Place margarine in sauce pan; melt over medium heat. Add onion; saute until tender. Stir in flour; add milk. Cook over medium heat; stir until thick and bubbly. Stir in spinach and pimiento.

Spoon spinach mixture over chicken; sprinkle with remaining cheese mixture. Cover; cook at 350° until Vapo-Valve "clicks." Reduce heat to 225°. Cover; cook 40-60 minutes.

Serves 6

To bone a chicken breast, remove the skin. Starting to one side of the breast bone, use a thin sharp knife to cut meat away from the bone. Continue cutting, using a sawing motion. Press the flat side of the knife against the rib bones. As you cut, use the other hand to pull the meat up and away from the rib bones.

Sauteed Chicken Breast

Utensil: 11" skillet

2 boneless, skinless chicken breast halves
1 tbsp sunflower oil
¼ cup flour
½ lemon; juiced
3 tbsp minced fresh parsley

Place chicken breast halves, one at a time, between 2 layers of waxed paper. Using food masher or rubber mallet, pound breasts until well flattened, but not broken apart.

Pour oil in skillet; preheat on medium. Dust chicken breasts with flour to lightly coat. Place chicken breasts in skillet. Saute breasts 10 minutes per side.

Remove chicken breasts to serving platter. Sprinkle with lemon juice; top with parsley.

Serves 2

Chicken breasts should just feel springy to the touch. If they are soft, the breasts are undercooked. If they are too hard, they are overcooked.

Chicken and Snow Peas

Utensil: Wok

½ lb fresh snow peas
3 boneless, skinless chicken breasts; cubed
2 tbsp sesame seed oil
1 (3 oz) pkg stir-fry season mix

Remove ends and "strings" from snow peas.

Preheat wok on medium-high. Add chicken; stir-fry until pink coloring disappears. DO NOT OVERCOOK CHICKEN. Add oil and season mix; blend well. Add snow peas; cook 5 minutes. Serve with rice.

Serves 6

Chicken Tetrazini

Utensils: 11" skillet, Saladmaster Food Processor

1   onion
2   stalks celery
1   (10 oz) box angel hair spaghetti
1   2-3 lb chicken; pre-cooked, de-boned
1   tbsp margarine
1   (10½ oz) can cream of mushroom soup
1   cup skim milk
½   bell pepper
1   (7 oz) jar chopped pimientos
1   (4½ oz) jar whole mushrooms
1   (10 oz) box Velveeta cheese; sliced

Cut onion using #2 Stringer food processor cone. Chop celery using #4 Thin Slicer cone.

Cook spaghetti according to package directions. Cut chicken into bite-size pieces.

Place margarine in skillet; melt over medium heat. Add onion and celery; saute until tender. Add chicken, mushroom soup, milk, bell pepper, pimientos and mushrooms. Cover; heat thoroughly at medium. Reduce heat to low; add sliced cheese. Cover; simmer until cheese is melted.

Gently mix all ingredients into spaghetti.

Serves 4

Lime-Sauced Chicken

Utensils: 11" skillet, 2-qt stainless steel bowl

4   boneless, skinless chicken breast halves
½   lime
¾   cup apple juice
2   tsp cornstarch
½   tsp instant chicken bouillon

Preheat skillet on medium. Add chicken. Cook 8-10 minutes; brown evenly on both sides. Remove from skillet; keep warm.

Remove thin strips of peel from lime. Reserve 1 tbsp juice.

In bowl combine lime juice, apple juice, cornstarch and bouillon; carefully add to skillet. Cook over medium heat; stir until thick and bubbly. Cook and stir 2 minutes.

To serve, cut each chicken breast half into 1" diagonal pieces. Spoon sauce over each serving. Garnish with reserved lime peel.

Serves 4

Raspberry Chicken

Utensils: 11" skillet, 1-qt sauce pan

1   cup fresh or frozen raspberries
1   tsp finely grated orange peel
½   cup orange juice
½   tsp instant chicken bouillon
⅛   tsp ground nutmeg
⅛   tsp black pepper
4   boneless, skinless chicken breast halves
2   tsp cornstarch
1   tbsp cold water
2½ tbsp honey

Thaw raspberries if frozen; set aside.

In skillet combine orange peel, orange juice, bouillon, nutmeg and pepper. Bring to boil over medium heat. Reduce heat to low; add chicken. Cover; simmer 10 minutes or until chicken is tender and no longer pink. Turn chicken; cook 5 minutes.

In sauce pan stir together cornstarch, water and honey. Cook over medium heat; stir until thick and bubbly. Gently stir in raspberries; heat thoroughly. Pour over chicken; serve with rice.

Serves 4

Baked Lemon Chicken

Utensil: 11" skillet

6   boneless, skinless chicken breasts
¼   tsp paprika
1   lemon

Place chicken breasts in skillet; sprinkle with paprika. Squeeze fresh lemon juice over chicken. Cover; cook at medium heat until Vapo-Valve "clicks." Reduce heat to low; simmer 25-30 minutes or until chicken is tender.

Serves 4-6

Crunchy Chicken Fingers

NOTE: *Excess fat is easily removed from chicken breasts with Saladmaster Shears.*

Utensils: Electric skillet, 1-qt and 2-qt stainless steel bowls

⅓ cup cornflake crumbs
½ cup finely chopped pecans
1 tbsp parsley flakes
¼ tsp garlic powder
2 tbsp skim milk
4 boneless, skinless chicken breasts; cut into strips
1 tbsp safflower oil

In 2-qt bowl combine cornflake crumbs, pecans, parsley and garlic powder. Pour milk into 1-qt bowl. Dip chicken strips in milk; coat with crumb mixture.

Pour safflower oil in electric skillet; heat at 375°. Place battered chicken in skillet; brown 4-5 minutes. Reduce heat to 275°. Cook until chicken turns loose from skillet; turn. Cover; cook 5-6 minutes until tender.

Serves 4

Chicken Cordon Bleu

Utensil: Electric skillet

8 boneless, skinless chicken breasts
1 large lemon
8 slices cured ham
8 slices lite Swiss cheese

Preheat electric skillet at 325°. Place chicken breasts in skillet; squeeze ½ lemon over chicken. Brown 5 minutes; turn. Squeeze other half of lemon on chicken; cook 3 minutes. Cover each chicken breast with slice of ham; top with cheese. Cover; cook 3-5 minutes or until cheese is melted.

Serves 8

Chicken Marsala

Utensil: 11" skillet

4   boneless, skinless chicken breast halves
1½ cups sliced fresh mushrooms
2   tbsp sliced green onion
2   tbsp water
¼   tsp salt substitute
¼   cup Marsala wine or dry sherry

Place one piece of chicken between two pieces of waxed paper. Working from the center to the edges, pound lightly with meat mallet to about ¼" thickness. Remove waxed paper. Repeat with remaining chicken breast halves.

Preheat skillet over medium heat. Add chicken breast halves. Cook 5-6 minutes or until chicken is tender and no longer pink. Transfer to platter; keep warm.

Carefully add mushrooms, green onion, water and salt substitute to skillet. Cook over medium heat 3 minutes or until mushrooms are tender and most of liquid has evaporated. Add Marsala wine or sherry to skillet; heat thoroughly on medium. Spoon vegetables and sauce over chicken.

Serves 4

Chicken Divan

Utensils: Electric skillet, 2-qt stainless steel bowl

1   (10¾ oz) can broccoli cheese soup
⅓   cup skim milk
1½ cups cubed, cooked chicken
4   cups steamed broccoli (page 88)
2   tbsp bread crumbs; toasted

In bowl combine soup and milk.

In electric skillet arrange chicken and broccoli. Top with soup mixture and bread crumbs. Cover; cook 15 minutes at 350°.

Serves 4

Italian Chicken

Utensils: 11" skillet, 1-qt stainless steel bowl

4 boneless, skinless chicken breasts
1 bell pepper; chopped
1 (8 oz) can tomato sauce
1 tbsp oregano
3 tbsp cornstarch
⅓ cup cold water
3 cups cooked rice (page 97)

Wash chicken; pat dry with paper towel. Preheat skillet on medium. Arrange chicken, skin side down, in skillet; press flat. Brown 10 minutes. Turn; brown other side 10 minutes.

In bowl combine bell pepper, tomato sauce and oregano; pour over chicken. Cover; cook over medium heat until Vapo-Valve "clicks." Reduce heat to low; cook 40-60 minutes. Uncover; remove chicken.

In bowl mix cornstarch and water; stir into sauce. Cook over low heat until thick, stirring occasionally. Serve chicken over rice; top with sauce.

Serves 4

Sweet-N-Sour Chicken

Utensil: Wok

4 boneless, skinless chicken breasts; cubed
1 (8 oz) can pineapple chunks; drained
1 (6 oz) bottle maraschino cherries; drained
1 (11½ oz) bottle sweet-and-sour sauce

Preheat wok on medium-high. Place cubed chicken in wok; cook 3-4 minutes. DO NOT OVERCOOK. Add pineapple, cherries and sauce; cook until hot. Serve with rice.

Serves 4

Chicken Chow Mein

Utensils: 4-qt roaster, 6-qt Dutch oven,
1-qt sauce pan, Saladmaster Food Processor

¼ lb fresh mushrooms; coarsely chopped
1 onion; chopped
¾ cup thinly sliced celery
1 carrot; scraped and grated
1 (3-3½ lb) fryer chicken; cut, skinned
2 chicken bouillon cubes
1 bell pepper; cut into strips
1 (14 oz) can bean sprouts; drained
1 (8 oz) can sliced water chestnuts; drained
1 (2 oz) jar diced pimiento; drained
2 tbsp lite soy sauce
1 tsp hot sauce
3 tbsp cornstarch
¼ cup water
1 (5 oz) can chow mein noodles
6 cups cooked rice (page 97)

Chop mushrooms and onion, slice celery and grate carrot using #2 Stringer food processor cone.

Place chicken in roaster. Cover; cook over medium heat until Vapo-Valve "clicks." Reduce heat to low; cook 45 minutes. Remove chicken; let cool slightly. De-bone chicken, cutting meat into bite-size pieces; set aside. Reserve chicken broth and add water to make 4 cups.

In Dutch oven add bouillon cubes and reserved broth. Bring to boil over medium heat. Add onion, celery, carrot and mushrooms. Reduce heat to low; simmer 10 minutes or until vegetables are tender. Add bell pepper, bean sprouts, water chestnuts, pimiento, soy sauce and hot sauce; mix together.

Combine cornstarch with water; stir until smooth. Pour into Dutch oven. Cook over medium heat, stirring constantly, until thick and bubbly. Add chicken pieces; mix well. Serve over rice; top with noodles.

Serves 8-10

TO FREEZE:
Prepare Chicken Chow Mein as directed omitting rice and chow mein noodles. Place in two 1½-qt airtight plastic containers. Freeze.

Marinated Chicken Stir-Fry

*Utensils: Wok, Saladmaster Food Processor,
1-qt and 3-qt stainless steel bowls*

2 zucchini
2 tbsp lemon juice
2 tbsp water
1 tbsp olive oil
½ tsp dried tarragon; crushed
¼ tsp hot pepper sauce
1 clove garlic; minced
4 oz boneless, skinless chicken breast halves;
     cut into 1" cubes
1 green bell pepper; chopped
1 red bell pepper; chopped

Cut zucchini using #5 Waffler food processor cone.

In 1-qt bowl combine lemon juice, water, oil, tarragon, hot pepper sauce and garlic. Place chicken breasts in 3-qt bowl. Pour marinade over chicken. Cover; let chicken marinate 20 minutes at room temperature.

Preheat wok over medium-high. Add chicken; reserve marinade. Cook until chicken is tender and no longer pink. Pull chicken to sides of wok. Add zucchini, green pepper, red pepper and ¼ cup marinade; stir-fry until vegetables are tender. Mix with chicken. Serve over rice.

Serves 4

Stir-Fry Chicken Dinner

Utensil: Wok

½   lb fresh snow peas
4   boneless, skinless chicken breasts
1   lb fresh broccoli; chopped
1   onion; thinly sliced
3   stalks celery; chopped
1   zucchini squash; sliced
1   bell pepper; sliced
6   large mushrooms; sliced
2   tbsp cornstarch
1¼ cups Sweet and Sour Sauce (page 34)
6   cups cooked rice (page 97)

Remove ends and "strings" from snow peas. Cut chicken breasts into 1" wide strips, about 2" long.

Preheat wok on medium-high heat. Place chicken breasts in wok. Cover; brown 2 minutes each side. Add broccoli and onion. Cover; cook 3 minutes. Add remaining vegetables; stir well. Cover; cook at medium until Vapo-Valve "clicks." Reduce heat to medium-low; cook 10 minutes.

Remove cover; push chicken/vegetables onto sides of wok. Add cornstarch and Sweet and Sour Sauce to liquid in bottom of wok; stir well. Mix into chicken/vegetables. Turn off heat. Cover; let stand 2 minutes. Serve over rice.

Serves 8-10

Selection of vegetables can be changed to individual liking. Fresh produce enhances flavor and nutritional value.

Crabmeat Chicken Rolls

Utensils: Electric skillet, 3-qt stainless steel bowl

1   (6 oz) can crabmeat
¼   cup finely chopped water chestnuts
2   tbsp fine dry bread crumbs
2   tbsp lite mayonnaise
1   tbsp snipped fresh parsley
¼   tsp Dijon mustard
6   boneless, skinless chicken breast halves
⅛   tsp lemon pepper
2   tbsp white wine Worcestershire sauce
3   green onions; chopped
⅛   tsp paprika

In bowl combine crabmeat, water chestnuts, bread crumbs, mayonnaise, parsley and mustard.

Place one piece of chicken between two pieces of waxed paper. Working from the center to the edges, pound lightly with meat mallet to ⅛″ thickness. Remove waxed paper and repeat with remaining chicken.

Sprinkle chicken with lemon pepper. Spoon crabmeat filling onto one end of each chicken breast half. Fold in sides; roll up. Arrange chicken in electric skillet, seam side down. Brush with 1 tbsp Worcestershire sauce. Cover; cook at 350° until Vapo-Valve "clicks." Reduce heat to 200°; simmer 20-25 minutes or until chicken is no longer pink. Brush with remaining Worcestershire sauce; sprinkle with green onions and paprika.

Serves 6

Oriental Poached Fish

Utensils: 11" skillet, 1-qt stainless steel bowl

- 2 tbsp lite French dressing
- 4 tsp lite soy sauce
- ¾ tsp ground ginger
- 1 lb flounder filets

In bowl combine French dressing, soy sauce and ginger; mix well.

Arrange fish fillets in cold skillet. Pour dressing mixture over fish. Marinate 10 minutes. Cover; cook on medium until Vapo-Valve "clicks." Reduce heat; cook 8-10 minutes until fish flakes. Pour sauce over fish servings.

Serves 4

Orange Roughy

Utensil: 11" skillet

- 3 fillets orange roughy
- 3 lemon slices
- 3 slices fresh tomatoes
- 3 rings bell pepper

Place fish in skillet. Top each fillet with slice of lemon, slice of tomato and slice of bell pepper. Cover; cook on medium heat until Vapo-Valve "clicks." Turn off heat; let stand 3-5 minutes, covered.

Serves 3

Stir-Fried Shrimp

Utensils: Wok, Saladmaster Food Processor

2 cloves garlic
3 cups fresh mushrooms
1 lb medium raw shrimp
2 tsp vegetable oil
1 cup sliced green onions
¼ cup dry white wine
2 cups cooked rice (page 97)

Finely grate garlic using #1 Shredder food processor cone. Slice mushrooms using #4 Thin Slicer cone. Peel and de-vein shrimp.

Place oil in wok; heat at medium-high. Add garlic; cook 1 minute, stirring frequently. Add shrimp; stir-fry 1 minute. Add mushrooms, onions and wine; stir-fry 2 minutes or until shrimp are pink and vegetables are crisp/tender. Serve over rice.

Serves 4

Spanish Style Catfish

Utensil: 11″ skillet

1 tbsp margarine
1 whole catfish
1 lemon
1 onion; chopped
1 clove garlic; chopped
1 tomato; chopped
1 bell pepper; chopped
1 tsp snipped cilantro

Place margarine in skillet; melt over medium heat. Add catfish; brown one side 10 minutes. Reduce heat to low. Turn fish; squeeze lemon over fish. Top with onion, garlic, tomato and bell pepper. Sprinkle with cilantro. Cover; simmer 10 minutes.

Serves 2

Parmesan Perch

Utensils: Electric skillet, 2-qt stainless steel bowl

1   lb ocean perch
2   tbsp dry bread crumbs
1   tbsp grated Parmesan cheese
1   tsp dried basil leaves
½   tsp paprika
⅛   tsp freshly ground black pepper
1   tbsp margarine; melted
2   tbsp chopped fresh parsley

Preheat electric skillet at 375°. Cut perch into 4 serving-size pieces.

In bowl mix bread crumbs, cheese, basil, paprika and pepper. Brush one side of fish with margarine; dip into crumb mixture. Place fish, uncoated side down, in skillet. Cover; cook 20 minutes or until fish flakes easily with fork. Sprinkle with parsley.

Serves 4

Eat a variety of foods. No one food provides all the nutrients that a person needs. It is important to eat a wide variety of foods each day such as: fruits and vegetables; whole grain breads and cereals; lean meats, poultry, and fish; dry peas and beans; and low-fat dairy products.

Red Snapper Almondine

½ lemon
4 red snapper fillets
1 cup flour
1 tbsp margarine; melted
⅛ tsp paprika
Shaved almonds

Squeeze lemon juice over fillets. Dip in flour; shake off excess flour. Place fillets in electric skillet. Pour margarine over fish; sprinkle with paprika. Cover; cook 10 minutes at 350°. Reduce heat to 275°; cook 10 minutes. Remove from skillet; place on serving dish. Add margarine drippings and almonds to top of each fillet before serving.

Serves 4

Fish contains about ⅔ the calories in an equal serving of red meat. Most fish is low in fat; and the fat it does contain is a poly-unsaturate called Omega-3. Omega-3 fights heart disease by changing the chemistry of blood so it is less likely to form artery-clogging clots. Omega-3 is found in salmon, mackerel, trout and haddock.

Crispy Baked Fillets

Utensil: Electric skillet

1 lb fish fillets
2 tbsp canola oil
⅓ cup cornflake crumbs
⅛ tsp freshly ground black pepper

Wash and dry fillets; cut into serving-size pieces. Dip in oil; coat with cornflake crumbs. Season with pepper. Arrange in electric skillet. Cover; cook 10 minutes at 325°. Reduce heat to 275°; cook 10 minutes.

Serves 4

Pan Fried Fish Fillets

Utensils: 11" skillet, 2-qt stainless steel bowl

⅓ cup flour
3 tbsp corn meal
1 tsp salt substitute
1½ lbs fish fillets
3 tbsp margarine

In bowl combine flour, corn meal and salt substitute. Dredge fish in flour mixture to coat both sides. Place margarine in skillet; melt over medium heat. Place coated fish in skillet; cook 5 minutes each side or until flaky.

Serves 4

Omelette Quiche

Utensils: 11" skillet, Saladmaster Food Processor

1 onion; chopped
1 cup grated Cheddar cheese
1 tbsp canola oil
6 eggs
2 tbsp water
1 bell pepper; diced
1 tomato; chopped
1 cup diced ham

Chop onions using #2 Stringer food processor cone. Grate cheese using #1 Shredder cone.

Pour canola oil into skillet; heat at medium. Add eggs, water, bell pepper, tomato, onion, cheese and ham; mix together. Cover; cook over medium heat 8-10 minutes. Reduce heat to low; cook 10 minutes.

Serves 3-4

Scrambled Eggs

*Utensils: 11" skillet, Saladmaster Food Processor,
2-qt stainless steel bowl*

¼ cup grated Cheddar cheese
4 eggs (or egg substitute)
1 green onion; chopped
½ bell pepper; chopped

Grate cheese using #1 Shredder food processor cone.

In bowl mix eggs, cheese, green onion and bell pepper. Pour into skillet. Cover; cook on medium heat until Vapo-Valve "clicks." Reduce heat to low; cook 2 minutes.

Serves 2

Hard or Soft Cooked Eggs

Utensil: 1-qt sauce pan

  3 eggs

Soak 2 paper towels in cold water. Place in bottom of sauce pan. Place eggs on paper towel; cover.

For soft cooked eggs, cook over medium heat until Vapo-Valve "clicks." For hard cooked eggs, cook over medium heat 15 minutes.

Serves 3

Greaseless Fried Eggs

Utensil: 11″ skillet

  2 tbsp water
  4 eggs

Preheat skillet over medium heat. Add water and eggs; season to taste. Cover; reduce heat to low. Cook 3 minutes for soft-yolk eggs, 4 minutes for hard-yolk eggs.

Serves 2

When cooking the Saladmaster way, always use the smallest pan to accommodate food. Different vegetables can be fixed in the same pan without mixing either flavor or color. Hard cooked eggs can be cooked along with vegetables. Rinse off eggs and lay on top of vegetables so that the eggs touch the pan.

French Toast

Utensils: 11" griddle, 3-qt stainless steel bowl

    Vegetable cooking spray
6 eggs (or egg substitute)
½ tsp cinnamon
¼ cup milk
10 slices bread

Spray griddle with cooking spray; preheat over medium heat.

In bowl mix eggs, cinnamon and milk. Dip bread slices into egg batter; place onto griddle. Cook until golden brown on both sides.

Serves 4-6

Cheese Omelette

Utensils: 10" gourmet skillet, Saladmaster Food Processor, 2-qt stainless steel bowl

½ cup Monterey Jack cheese
½ cup Cheddar cheese
    Vegetable cooking spray
5 eggs (or egg substitute)

Grate cheeses using #1 Shredder food processor cone.

Lighly spray skillet with cooking spray; preheat over medium heat.

In bowl lightly whip eggs. Pour eggs into skillet; cook 5 minutes or until sides of omelette are lightly brown. Add cheese to omelette; fold in half. Cook 3-5 minutes.

Serves 3

Greaseless Pancakes

Utensils: 11" griddle, 3-qt stainless steel bowl

2   eggs (or egg substitute)
2   tbsp sugar
1   tbsp margarine; melted
2   cups skim milk
2½   cups flour
3   tbsp baking powder

In bowl place eggs and sugar; beat until thick. Add margarine and skim milk. Sift flour and baking powder together; stir into egg mixture.

Preheat griddle over medium heat. For each pancake pour about 3 tbsp batter onto skillet. Cook pancakes until puffed and dry around edges. Turn; cook other side until golden brown.

Serves 6

Potato Pancakes

Utensils: 11" skillet, Saladmaster Food Processor, 3-qt stainless steel bowl

3   potatoes
1   onion
2   eggs (or egg substitute)
⅛   tsp black pepper
3   tbsp skim milk
⅓   cup flour
½   tsp baking powder
2   tbsp margarine; melted

Cut potatoes and onion using #1 Shredder food processor cone. Preheat skillet over medium heat.

Place eggs in bowl; beat. Add remaining ingredients; mix well. Drop batter, by large spoonfuls, into skillet. Brown each side. Cover; reduce heat to low. Cook 2 minutes.

Serves 6

For a healthier breakfast, you should choose more fruits and whole grain cereals. When making pancakes and waffles, use whole wheat flour instead of white flour and one whole egg plus one egg white, rather than two whole eggs. For a low fat topping with fiber, try applesauce, apple butter and cinnamon.

Oatmeal Pancakes with Strawberry Sauce

Utensils: 11" griddle, 2-qt and 3-qt stainless steel bowls

	Vegetable cooking spray
1½	cups uncooked regular oats
½	cup flour
1	tbsp baking powder
¼	tsp salt substitute
1¼	cups skim milk
2	egg whites; slightly beaten
2	tbsp corn oil
2	cups strawberry sauce (page 82)

Spray griddle with cooking spray; preheat over medium heat.

In 3-qt bowl place oats, flour, baking powder and salt substitute; mix well. Form a "well" in center of mixture. In 2-qt bowl combine milk, egg whites and oil; stir until well blended. Pour into dry ingredients; combine until moistened.

For each pancake pour 3 tbsp batter onto hot griddle; smooth to distribute oats. Turn pancakes when tops are covered with bubbles and edges are lightly browned. Top each serving of pancakes with ¼ cup strawberry sauce. Serve immediately.

Makes 1 dozen pancakes

Strawberry Sauce

Utensils: 1-qt sauce pan

4 cups fresh strawberries; washed, hulled, halved
½ cup sugar
½ cup + 2 tbsp orange juice; divided
1 tsp lemon juice
1½ tsp cornstarch

Combine 2 cups halved strawberries, sugar, 2 tbsp orange juice and lemon juice in sauce pan. Cook over medium heat, stirring constantly, 3-5 minutes or until sugar dissolves and strawberries begin to soften. Remove from heat; transfer mixture to container of electric blender. Cover; process until slightly pureed.

Combine cornstarch and remaining ½ cup orange juice in sauce pan; stir until dissolved. Add pureed strawberry mixture; cook over medium heat, stirring frequently, 5 minutes or until clear and slightly thickened. Remove from heat; stir in remaining strawberries. Serve warm over pancakes, or let cool to serve as topping for fresh fruit or desserts. Store in an airtight container.

Makes 3 cups

Basic Crepes

Utensils: 9" skillet, 3-qt stainless steel bowl

NOTE: *To make dessert crepes, follow this basic crepe recipe with the following exceptions: Mix 1 tsp sugar with flour and add 1 tsp vanilla to milk. Mix as directed.*

Leftovers make a great filler for the next meal. Just use them in an omelette or crepe and no one will ever know they are leftovers. This is an especially good idea for cheese, green vegetables, tomatoes and any kind of red meat. Seafood makes an especially tempting filler.

1 cup flour
¼ tsp salt substitute
3 eggs
¼ cup water
1 cup milk
1 tbsp margarine; melted
   Vegetable cooking spray

In bowl combine flour and salt substitute. Add eggs; beat well after each addition. Gradually stir in water, milk and margarine; mix well. Cover bowl; let batter set 1-2 hours at room temperature. Flour will expand and thicken batter.

Spray underside of skillet with cooking spray. Preheat skillet, bottom side up, over medium-high heat 3-5 minutes or until a drop of water sizzles off surface.

Pour batter into large dinner plate to a depth of ¾". Hold pan in level position; dip into batter so bottom is covered. Lift pan; turn batter side up. Swirl pan so excess batter fills in any holes or spaces. Place skillet, bottom side up, on the burner. Cook over medium heat until golden brown around edge. Remove crepe from pan bottom; place browned side down on plate. To keep crepes moist, cover immediately. Repeat until all batter is used. Lightly spray bottom of skillet with cooking spray if sticking occurs.

Makes 18 crepes

Easy Vegetable Crepes

Utensils: 1-qt sauce pan, pudding pan

1   (13½ oz) can Cheddar cheese soup
8   crepes (page 83)
2½ lbs asparagus spears; cooked, drained
8   slices bacon; fried
    Vegetable cooking spray

In sauce pan heat soup on medium 5 minutes. Place crepes, browned side down, on waxed paper. Place three asparagus spears in center of each crepe. Top with one strip bacon. Spoon 2 tbsp of cheese soup over bacon. Fold crepes in thirds.

Spray pudding pan with cooking spray. Place crepes in pudding pan; bake in oven 15 minutes at 325°. Remove from oven; top with remaining cheese soup.

Serves 4-6

VARIATION:
Substitute 2½ lbs whole cooked green beans and cream of mushroom soup for asparagus and Cheddar cheese soup.

Breakfast Crepes

Utensils: 11″ skillet, high dome cover, 3-qt stainless steel bowl

1   tbsp margarine
8   eggs
½   cup milk
1   cup diced ham
8   crepes (page 83)
1   cup grated Cheddar cheese

Place margarine in skillet; melt over medium heat. In bowl beat together eggs and milk. Pour eggs into skillet; stir in ham. Cook over medium heat, stirring occasionally, until eggs are set. Place crepes, browned side down, on waxed paper. Place about ⅓ cup egg mixture in center of each crepe; top with 1 tbsp cheese. Fold crepes in thirds; place in high dome cover. Sprinkle remaining cheese over crepes. Bake in preheated oven 10-15 minutes at 325°.

Serves 4

Seafood Crepes

Utensils: 9" skillet, 2-qt and 3-qt stainless steel bowls

2 (6 oz) pkgs frozen crabmeat; flaked
½ cup sliced celery
3 tbsp sliced green onions
1 (8 oz) can water chestnuts; drained, diced
1 (6 oz) pkg frozen cocktail shrimp; divided
½ cup lite mayonnaise
2 tbsp skim milk
3 tbsp chili sauce
½ tsp Worcestershire sauce
1 tsp onion salt
12 crepes (page 83)

In 2 qt bowl combine crabmeat, celery, onions, water chestnuts and one-half of shrimp. Cover; chill 1 hour.

In 3 qt bowl combine mayonnaise, milk, chili sauce, Worcestershire sauce and onion salt; mix thoroughly. Gently stir in remaining shrimp. Cover; chill 1 hour.

Place crepes, browned side down, on waxed paper. Spoon 2 tbsp crabmeat filling in middle of each crepe; fold crepes in thirds. Arrange on serving dish; spoon sauce over crepes.

Serves 6-8

Enchilada Bake

Utensils: Electric skillet, 10" gourmet skillet,
Saladmaster Food Processor, 1-qt stainless steel bowl

1	clove garlic; minced
1	onion; chopped
¼	cup grated mozzarella cheese
6	mushrooms; sliced
1	bell pepper; chopped
1	tbsp margarine
1	(16 oz) can pinto beans
1	(14½ oz) can stewed tomatoes
1	tbsp chili powder
1	tsp ground cumin
½	cup dry white wine
½	cup ricotta cheese
¼	cup low-fat plain yogurt
8	whole wheat corn tortillas
6	black olives

Mince garlic using #1 Shredder food processor cone. Chop onion and grate cheese using #2 Stringer cone. Slice mushrooms using #4 Thin Slicer cone.

Place margarine in gourmet skillet; melt over medium heat. Add onion, garlic, mushrooms and bell pepper; saute until tender. Add beans, tomatoes, spices and wine. Cover; reduce heat to low. Simmer 30 minutes.

In bowl mix ricotta cheese and yogurt.

In electric skillet put layer of tortillas, layer of sauce, 1½ tbsp of grated cheese and 4 tbsp of cheese/yogurt mixture. Repeat until all tortillas are used, ending with layer of sauce. Top with cheese/yogurt mixture and black olives. Cover; cook at 350° until Vapo-Valve "clicks." Reduce heat to low; simmer 15-20 minutes.

Serves 6

Vegetables

Carrots

Utensils: 2-qt sauce pan, Saladmaster Food Processor

4   medium carrots

Cut carrots using #2 Stringer food processor cone. Rinse in cold water; drain. Place in sauce pan; cook on medium heat. When Vapo-Valve "clicks," reduce heat to low. Cook 10 minutes.

Serves 4

Steamed Fresh Broccoli or Cauliflower

Utensils: 3-qt sauce pan, steamer inset

1   lb fresh broccoli or cauliflower
4   cups water

Wash broccoli or cauliflower; place in steamer inset. Pour water in sauce pan; boil at medium heat. Insert steamer into sauce pan. Cover; steam 12-15 minutes.

Serves 4

Fresh Beets

Utensils: 2-qt saucepan, Saladmaster Food Processor

3   fresh beets
1   (16 oz) can cranberry sauce
2   tbsp orange juice

Wash beets; cut in half. Slice beets using #2 Stringer food processor cone, making sure peeling side is away from cone. Place beets in sauce pan; heat at medium until Vapo-Valve "clicks." Reduce heat to low; cook 15-20 minutes. Add cranberry sauce and orange juice; simmer 5 minutes.

Serves 4

To keep bright colors in your vegetables, follow a few simple rules: (1) Do not use water or salt - both rob vital nutrients. (2) Cook vegetables over low heat. (3) Do not overcook. Overcooked cauliflower turns from white to an unappealing brownish-gray. Green vegetables become a dull olive color.

By keeping cooking times brief, using low heat and no water, you will not only preserve appetizing colors, but valuable nutrients, as well. Strongly flavored vegetables such as Brussel sprouts, broccoli, cauliflower and turnips become stronger when overcooked because they release sulfur compounds.

Lima Beans

Utensil: 3-qt sauce pan

These are the top sources for Vitamin E:

• *Oils*
• *Nuts*
• *Corn*
• *Lima beans*

1 (1 lb) pkg dry lima beans
6 cups water

Rinse lima beans; place in sauce pan. Pour in 3 cups water; soak overnight.

Drain beans; add 3 cups water. Cover; cook at medium until Vapo-Valve "clicks." Reduce heat to low; cook 45 minutes or until beans are tender.

Serves 4

French Cut Beans Almondine

Utensils: 9" skillet, 3-qt sauce pan

1 lb fresh green beans
¼ cup sliced almonds
2 tbsp minced fresh parsley

Prepare green beans by cutting 2" pieces on very sharp diagonal.

Place almonds in skillet; stir over low heat until lightly browned. Set aside; let pan cool completely. Rinse and drain green beans; place in sauce pan. Cover; cook over medium heat. When Vapo-Valve "clicks," reduce heat to low. Cook 8-10 minutes or until beans are firm/tender. Add almonds and parsley; mix well.

Serves 4

Corn on the Cob

Utensil: 11" skillet

FROZEN

6   ears sweet corn

Preheat skillet on medium. Moisten paper towel; place in bottom of skillet. Place corn on paper towel. Cover; cook over medium heat until Vapo-Valve "clicks." Reduce heat to low; cook 12-15 minutes.

Serves 6

Utensils: 11" skillet, 11" utility rack, high dome cover

FRESH

4   ears sweet corn
4   cups water

Shuck sweet corn; cut in half and wash. Pour water into skillet; insert utility rack. Bring water to boil on medium heat. Place corn on rack; cover with high dome cover. Steam corn 20-30 minutes.

Serves 4

To freeze fresh corn, blanching is recommended. This process slows down the loss of essential vitamins and the heat from boiling helps maintain color while killing some micro-organisms on the corn.

Creamed
Mexican-Style Corn

Utensil: 2-qt sauce pan

1 (10 oz) pkg frozen whole kernel corn
¼ cup chopped green bell pepper
¼ cup chopped red bell pepper
¼ cup chopped celery
¼ cup lite cream cheese
¼ cup diced green chili peppers
1 tbsp skim milk

In sauce pan combine corn, green pepper, red pepper and celery. Cover; cook 5-10 minutes at medium-low heat. Drain.

Stir in cream cheese, chili peppers and milk. Heat 5 minutes at medium-low.

Serves 4

Butternut Squash

Utensils: 8" skillet, Saladmaster Food Processor

2   large butternut squash
1   tbsp margarine
½   tsp nutmeg
½   tsp cinnamon

Quarter squash lengthwise; remove seeds. Cut squash using #1 Shredder food processor cone, keeping rind away from cone to peel. Place squash in skillet. Cover; cook 15 minutes at medium-low heat. Add margarine, nutmeg and cinnamon.

Serves 4

Stuffed Winter Squash

Utensils: 3-qt sauce pan, steamer inset, Saladmaster Food Processor, 3-qt stainless steel bowl

1   oz fresh Parmesan cheese
½   onion
½   zucchini
½   carrot
1   apple
½   tsp dried tarragon
⅛   tsp freshly ground black pepper
1   acorn or butternut squash; halved, seeded
4   cups water

Grate cheese using #1 Shredder food processor cone. Cut onion using #2 Stringer cone. Grate zucchini and carrot and cut apple using #3 French Fryer cone.

In bowl mix zucchini, carrot, apple, onion, cheese, tarragon and pepper. Stuff squash halves with vegetable mixture; place in steamer inset. Pour water in sauce pan; bring to boil over medium heat. Insert steamer into sauce pan. Cover; steam until Vapo-Valve "clicks." Reduce heat to low; steam 20 minutes.

Serves 2

The National Cancer Institute recommends that you eat a variety of foods rich in vitamins rather than relying on vitamin supplements. Good sources of Vitamin A include the following yellow-orange vegetables and fruits:

- Carrots
- Winter squash
- Sweet potatoes
- Pumpkins
- Peaches
- Cantaloupes
- Mangoes

Herbed Vegetable Toss

Utensils: 3-qt sauce pan, steamer inset

- 4 cups water
- 12 whole new potatoes
- 4 medium carrots; bias-sliced into 1" pieces
- 2 tsp olive oil
- ¼ tsp dried rosemary or thyme; crushed

Pour water into sauce pan; bring to boil over medium heat. Insert steamer into sauce pan.

Peel a ½" strip around the center of each new potato. Place potatoes and carrots in steamer. Cover; steam 20-25 minutes or until vegetables are tender. Remove vegetables from steamer; place in serving bowl. Sprinkle with oil and rosemary or thyme. Toss lightly to coat.

Serves 4

Frozen Vegetables . . . The Waterless Way

Utensil: 2-qt sauce pan

- 1 (10 oz) pkg frozen vegetable, such as broccoli, peas, carrots, corn

Place frozen vegetable in sauce pan. Cover; cook over medium heat until Vapo-Valve "clicks." Reduce heat to low; simmer 15-20 minutes.

Serves 4

Stir-Fry Vegetables

Utensil: Wok

3 tbsp lemon juice
2 tbsp sesame seed oil
1 tbsp sesame seeds
2 tbsp lite soy sauce
2 tbsp garlic powder
   Variety of vegetables such as: broccoli, green bell peppers, yellow bell peppers, red bell peppers, scallions, carrots, water chestnuts, Chinese cabbage, snow peas, baby corn

Preheat wok on medium-high. Add ingredients; stir-fry 7-10 minutes. Serve with rice (page 97).

Serving size will vary depending on amount of vegetables used.

Fresh vegetables . . . including the peel . . . are an excellent source of vitamins and minerals. Avoid pre-processed canned or frozen vegetables.

- Don't wash vegetables until ready to use. After thoroughly washing, most thin-skinned vegetables can be cooked unpared.
- Unless directed otherwise, never soak vegetables after they have been pared or sliced.
- To stir-fry properly . . . preserving nutrients, flavor and crispness . . . use medium-high heat and cook quickly.

Zucchini Lasagna

Utensil: Electric skillet

8   uncooked lasagna noodles
1   cup sliced fresh mushrooms
½   cup chopped onion
1   clove garlic; minced
3   cups thinly sliced zucchini
2   cups lite cottage cheese
1   (16 oz) jar prepared spaghetti sauce
½   cup grated fresh Parmesan cheese
1   cup grated mozzarella cheese

In cold electric skillet layer in the following order: 4 uncooked lasagna noodles, ½ cup mushrooms, ¼ cup onion, ½ clove garlic, 1½ cups zucchini, 1 cup cottage cheese, 8 oz spaghetti sauce, ¼ cup Parmesan cheese and ½ cup mozzarella cheese. Layer a second time. Cover; cook 40 minutes at 250°-275°.

Serves 8

Cabbage

Utensils: 2-qt sauce pan, Saladmaster Food Processor

6   cups cut cabbage
1   tsp lemon pepper
1   tsp butter (optional)

Cut cabbage using #4 Thin Slicer food processor cone.

Rinse cabbage in cold water; place in sauce pan. Cover; cook over medium heat until Vapo-Valve "clicks." Reduce heat to low; cook 10 minutes or until tender. Add lemon pepper and butter, if desired. Blend well.

Serves 6

Fresh Steamed Asparagus with Almonds

Utensils: 3-qt sauce pan, steamer inset, 8" gourmet skillet

2   lbs fresh asparagus
2   cups water
1   (2 oz) pkg slivered almonds
1   tsp margarine

Wash fresh asparagus and trim end of stems.

Pour water in sauce pan; bring to boil over medium heat. Place fresh asparagus in steamer; insert in sauce pan. Cover; steam 25 minutes or until tender.

Place margarine in skillet; melt over low heat. Add almonds; saute. Top fresh asparagus with sauteed almonds before serving.

Serves 4

Asparagus Casserole

Utensils: Electric skillet, 3-qt stainless steel bowl

1   (11 oz) can Cheddar cheese soup
1   cup sour cream
3   (15 oz) cans asparagus; drained
1   (6 oz) can French fried onions

In bowl dilute Cheddar cheese soup with sour cream. Place asparagus in skillet. Pour soup over asparagus. Cover; heat thoroughly 15-20 minutes at 250°. Sprinkle French fried onions on top of asparagus. Cook, uncovered, 5 minutes.

Serves 8

Basic Rice

Utensil: 2-qt sauce pan

1 cup rice; rinsed
2 cups water

Place rice in sauce pan; add water. Cover; cook at medium heat until Vapo-Valve "clicks." Reduce heat to low; cook 15 minutes.

Serves 6

Salt (sodium) can be entirely eliminated from any Saladmaster recipe. Here are some suggestions to reduce salt in your diet.

- *Use salt substitutes, herbs and spices to add zest and flavor to any dish.*
- *Use low-sodium or unsalted ingredients for cooking. Avoid processed foods.*
- *Reduce consumption of smoked, pickled and salted meats like ham, bacon, sausage. Instead use fresh meats, fish and poultry.*
- *Do not add salt to boiling water when cooking rice, pasta and vegetables.*

Creole Rice

Utensil: 3-qt sauce pan

2 (10 oz) cans tomatoes with green chili peppers; undrained
1½ cups water
2 tbsp margarine
1 tsp garlic powder
½ tsp dried parsley flakes
½ tsp dried whole oregano
¼ tsp salt
½ cup chopped bell pepper
½ cup chopped green onions
1 cup uncooked long-grain rice

Drain tomatoes; reserve 1 cup liquid. Combine tomato liquid, water, margarine, garlic powder, parsley flakes, oregano and salt in sauce pan. Bring mixture to boil over medium heat. Add tomatoes, bell pepper, green onions and rice. Cover; reduce heat to low. Simmer 20 minutes or until rice is tender and liquid is absorbed.

Serves 4-6

Orange Spiced Rice

Utensils: 3-qt sauce pan, Saladmaster Food Processor

1   onion
2   celery stalks
2   oranges
1   tbsp margarine
2   cups brown rice
3   cups water
2   cups chicken broth
⅔   cup golden raisins

Cut onion and celery using #1 Shredder food processor cone. Grate peel of 1 orange using #1 Shredder cone. Peel second orange; cut both oranges into small segments.

Place margarine in sauce pan; melt over low heat. Add onions and celery. Increase heat to medium; saute 3 minutes. Add rice; saute 2 minutes. Add water, broth, raisins and grated orange peel. Cover; bring to boil. When Vapo-Valve "clicks," reduce heat to low. Simmer 30-40 minutes. Add orange segments to rice. Serve immediately.

Serves 8

Waldorf Rice

Utensils: 11" skillet, Saladmaster Food Processor

2 celery stalks
½ cup toasted almonds
1 apple
¾ cup brown rice
1½ cups unsweetened apple juice
1 tbsp lemon juice

Chop celery and almonds using #2 Stringer food processor cone. Cut apple using #3 French Fryer cone.

Preheat skillet on medium heat. Add almonds; toast, stirring until golden brown. Remove; set aside.

Place rice in skillet. Toast over medium heat, stirring to prevent scorching. Reduce heat to low; slowly add apple and lemon juices. Cover; cook 15 minutes. Stir in celery. Cover; cook 5 minutes or until liquid is absorbed.

Add apple to rice; stir in almonds. Serve immediately.

Serves 6-8

Brown Rice Pilaf

Utensils: 2-qt sauce pan, Saladmaster Food Processor

½ cup shredded carrot
1 cup cut fresh mushrooms
½ tsp instant chicken bouillon
1 cup water
¾ cup quick-cooking brown rice
¼ tsp dried marjoram; crushed
⅛ tsp freshly ground black pepper
¼ cup thinly sliced green onion
2 tbsp snipped fresh parsley

Shred carrot using #1 Shredder food processor cone.
Cut mushrooms using #2 Stringer cone.

In sauce pan stir together bouillon and water. Bring
to boil over medium heat. Stir in mushrooms, brown
rice, carrot, marjoram and pepper. Cover; reduce heat
to low. Simmer 12 minutes. Remove from heat; let
stand 5 minutes. Add green onion and parsley; toss
lightly with fork. Serve immediately.

Serves 4

15-Minute Hash Browns

Utensils: Electric skillet, Saladmaster Food Processor

3 potatoes
3 tbsp canola oil

Cut potatoes using #1 Shredder food processor cone.

Pour canola oil into electric skillet; heat at 420°. Add potatoes, pushing potatoes away from sides of skillet. Cook, uncovered, 7 minutes or until golden brown. Turn; cook 7 minutes or until brown on other side.

Serves 6

Sweet Potatoes

Utensils: 8" skillet, Saladmaster Food Processor

3 medium sweet potatoes
½ cup packed brown sugar
⅓ cup miniature marshmallows

Wash sweet potatoes; cut using #5 Waffler food processor cone.

Place sweet potatoes in skillet. Cover; cook on medium heat until Vapo-Valve "clicks." Reduce heat to low; cook 30 minutes. Stir in brown sugar and marshmallows. Cover; cook 10 minutes.

Serves 6

Steamed Potatoes

Utensils: Steamer inset, 3-qt sauce pan, Saladmaster Food Processor

2 large potatoes
4 cups water

Cut potatoes using #3 French Fryer food processor cone.

Pour water into sauce pan; bring to boil over medium heat. Place potatoes in steamer; insert into sauce pan. Cover; steam 10-15 minutes.

Serves 4

Potato Salad

Utensils: 3-qt sauce pan, steamer inset,
2-qt and 3-qt stainless steel bowls

4	cups water
4	medium potatoes
2	tbsp lemon juice
1	tsp fresh dill weed
1	cucumber peeled; seeded, diced
1	medium bell pepper; seeded, diced
1	medium tomato; seeded, diced
½	cup lite creamy Italian dressing

Pour water into sauce pan; bring to boil over medium heat. Place potatoes in steamer; insert into sauce pan. Cover; steam 15 minutes or until potatoes are tender. Remove potatoes; cool. Peel and dice potatoes; place in 3-qt bowl.

In 2-qt bowl combine remaining ingredients; mix well. Add dressing mixture to potatoes; toss gently. Cover; chill 3 hours.

Serves 10

Top-of-Stove Baked Potatoes

Utensil: 11″ skillet

4	medium potatoes

Cut potatoes in half. Make a "cross" into meat side of each potato half; wipe dry with paper towel. Place meat side down in skillet. Cover; cook over medium heat until Vapo-Valve "clicks." Reduce heat to low; cook 30 minutes.

Serves 8

One baked potato has fewer calories than one-half cup of cottage cheese. Potatoes are 80 percent water, low in sodium and virtually fat free. Leaving the skins on potatoes is an excellent way to preserve nutrients.

Breads
&
Desserts

Whole Wheat Biscuits

Utensils: Electric skillet, 3-qt stainless steel bowl

1 cup whole wheat flour
1 cup all-purpose flour
1 tbsp baking powder
½ tsp salt
¾ cup skim milk
¼ cup canola oil
   Vegetable cooking spray

In bowl combine flours, baking powder and salt; stir well. Add milk and oil; stir to form soft dough.

Place dough onto lightly floured surface; knead lightly 2-3 times. Roll dough to ½" thickness; cut with biscuit cutter.

Spray electric skillet with cooking spray; preheat at 375°. Place cut biscuits into skillet. Reduce heat to 350°; bake uncovered 5-8 minutes or until golden brown. Turn; brown other side.

Makes 1 dozen biscuits

Breads that have a high fat content are croissants, doughnuts and sweet rolls. One four-inch croissant can contain as much as four teaspoons of butter.

Cheese & Vegetable Cornbread

*Utensils: 9" skillet, Saladmaster Food Processor,
3-qt stainless steel bowl*

¼ cup grated Cheddar cheese
1 tbsp chopped onion
1 cup flour
½ cup white cornmeal
1 tbsp sugar
1 tbsp baking powder
¾ cup skim milk
1 egg white; beaten
3 tbsp chopped bell pepper
1 tbsp melted margarine
 Vegetable cooking spray

Grate cheese using #1 Shredder food processor cone. Chop onion using #2 Stringer cone.

Combine flour, cornmeal, sugar and baking powder in bowl; stir well. Gradually add milk; stir well to mix. Add cheese, egg white, bell pepper, onion and margarine; stir gently to mix.

Lightly spray skillet with cooking spray; preheat at medium. Pour batter into skillet. Cover; cook 25 minutes. Cut into squares; serve hot.

Makes 9 servings

Spanish Cornbread

Utensils: Electric skillet, Saladmaster Food Processor, 3-qt stainless steel bowl

½ cup grated lite Cheddar cheese
1 cup cornmeal
½ tsp baking soda
½ tsp salt
1 cup canned cream-style corn
⅔ cup nonfat buttermilk
1 (4 oz) can green chilies; chopped, drained
2 egg whites; slightly beaten
1 tbsp canola oil
 Vegetable cooking spray

Grate cheese using #1 Shredder food processor cone.

Combine cornmeal, baking soda and salt in bowl; stir well. Add corn, buttermilk, chilies, egg whites and oil.

Spray electric skillet lightly with cooking spray; preheat at 375°. Spoon one-half of batter into hot skillet; sprinkle with cheese. Add remaining batter. Cover; cook 12 minutes at 250°.

Serves 6-8

Use the following chart for selecting breads:

- *1 plain bagel - 165 calories*
- *1 slice white bread - 75 calories*
- *1 slice whole wheat bread - 65 calories*
- *1 six-inch croissant - 246 calories*
- *1 yeast doughnut - 176 calories*
- *1 blueberry muffin - 112 calories*
- *1 bran muffin - 105 calories*
- *1 four-inch pancake - 70 calories*

Never Fail Pie Crust

Utensils: Two 9″ pie pans, 2-qt and 3-qt
stainless steel bowls

3 cups flour
1¼ cups lite shortening
1 tsp salt
1 egg; well beaten
5 tbsp water
1 tbsp vinegar

In 3-qt bowl place flour, shortening and salt. Cut shortening into flour and salt.

In 2-qt bowl combine egg, water and vinegar. Pour liquid into flour mixture. Blend with fork until flour is moistened. Divide dough in half; roll out flat. Place in pie pans; mold edge. Use fork to pierce dough to prevent shrinkage. Bake in oven 10-15 minutes at 350°. Cool.

Makes 2 crusts

When you shop for blueberries, make sure they have been refrigerated, look plump and firm, and have a powdery, greyish-blue color. To store blueberries, wrap tightly without washing. Wash berries just before eating. Moisture causes them to turn mushy.

Berry Pie

Utensil: 2-qt sauce pan

1 qt strawberries or raspberries
¾ cup sugar
2½ tbsp cornstarch
1 cup water
1 Never Fail Pie Crust; prepared with
    generous high rim

Clean and hull berries. In sauce pan blend 1 cup fruit. Add sugar, cornstarch and water. Cook, stirring until thick, over low heat 10-15 minutes. Put whole berries into pie shell; distribute evenly. Pour syrup over berries, coating them thoroughly by turning but not displacing them. Chill pie in refrigerator 4 hours. Serve garnished with whipped cream.

Chocolate Pie

Utensils: 3-qt sauce pan, 1-qt and 2-qt stainless steel bowls

1¾ cups sugar; divided
4 tbsp flour
½ cup cocoa
3 cups milk
4 eggs; separated
½ tsp vanilla
2 tbsp margarine
2 Never Fail Pie Crusts (page 107)

In sauce pan combine 1½ cups sugar, flour and cocoa. Gradually stir in milk. Cook over medium heat, stirring constantly, until mixture thickens. Boil 1 minute; remove from heat.

Beat egg yolks in 1-qt bowl. Slowly add ½ cup hot filling to yolks, stirring constantly. Add yolk mixture to remaining filling. Add vanilla and margarine; mix well. Pour mixture into pie crusts.

In 2-qt bowl beat egg whites until stiff peaks form. Gradually add ¼ cup sugar; continuing to beat. Spread meringue evenly on top of pie mixture, sealing edges. Bake in oven 8-10 minutes at 400° to brown meringue.

Makes two 9″ pies

Easy Chocolate Pie

Utensil: 1-qt sauce pan

1 (7½ oz) large Hershey almond bar
1 (8 oz) Cool Whip
1 Never Fail Pie Crust (page 107)

Melt chocolate in sauce pan on medium heat. Remove from heat. Fold in Cool Whip; mix well. Pour into pie crust. Refrigerate 1 hour.

Serves 6-8

Some recipes call for baking chocolate. It is healthier to substitute three tablespoons of cocoa plus one tablespoon of canola oil for each ounce of chocolate that the recipe requires. The substitution will reduce the total amount of fat, and the fat will be unsaturated rather than saturated.

108

Peach Pie

8 peaches; sliced
1 cup sugar
2 tbsp cornstarch
2 tbsp margarine
½ tsp vanilla
1 Never Fail Pie Crust (page 107)

Place half the peaches, sugar and cornstarch in sauce pan. Cook at medium heat until thick; stir constantly. Add margarine and vanilla. Cool mixture. Place remaining peach slices in pie crust. Pour peach mixture over top. Refrigerate 1 hour.

Serves 6-8

Skillet Chocolate Cake

Utensils: 11" skillet, 2-qt stainless steel bowl

For best flavor, remove chilled pies from refrigerator 20 minutes before serving to enhance taste.

Vegetable cooking spray
½ cup cocoa
⅓ cup water
1½ cups flour
1 tsp baking soda
1 cup brown sugar
½ cup margarine
3 eggs; unbeaten
½ cup buttermilk
1 tsp vanilla
2 (4 oz) bars sweet chocolate

Spray bottom and sides of skillet with cooking spray to prevent sticking. Preheat skillet over low heat.

In bowl dissolve cocoa in water. Add all remaining ingredients, except chocolate bars; mix until well blended. Pour batter into skillet. Break chocolate bars into small squares; arrange on top of batter. Cover; cook over low heat 40 minutes.

Serves 10-12

Pineapple Upside Down Cake

Utensils: Electric skillet, 3-qt stainless steel bowl

4 tbsp margarine
1 cup brown sugar
1 (16 oz) can sliced pineapple; drain, reserve juice
8 maraschino cherries
2 egg whites
2 Jiffy cake mixes

Place margarine in electric skillet; melt at 200°. Add brown sugar; stir into melted margarine. Spread mixture evenly over bottom of skillet. Place 8 pineapple slices symetrically in skillet. Place maraschino cherries in middle of each ring.

In bowl mix egg whites and cake mixes. Use reserved pineapple juice for liquid. Prepare according to cake mix directions.

Increase electric skillet heat to 350°. Pour batter into skillet over pineapple; cook 6-8 minutes. Reduce heat to 250°; cook 6-8 minutes or until cake is done. Shake skillet gently to loosen cake; turn upside down immediately onto cake plate.

Serves 6-8

Saladmaster Health Cake

Utensils: 3-qt stainless steel bowl, pudding pan, 6-qt Dutch oven, 11" utility rack, high dome cover, Saladmaster Food Processor

1 (1 lb) box Graham crackers
⅔ cup dates
½ cup pecans
2 tsp baking powder
2 eggs
2 cups skim milk
  Vegetable cooking spray
4 cups water

Crush Graham crackers and chop dates and pecans using #1 Shredder food processor cone.

In bowl mix Graham crackers and baking powder. Blend in eggs and milk. Add dates and nuts. Lightly spray pudding pan with cooking spray. Pour batter into pudding pan. Pour water into Dutch oven. Insert utility rack into Dutch oven; set pudding pan on rack. Cover; heat at medium 15 minutes. Reduce heat to medium-low; cook 1 hour. Cool; cover with sauce.

Sauce for Health Cake

Utensil: 1-qt sauce pan

1 cup water
1 cup sugar
1 tbsp cornstarch
1 lemon; juiced
1 tsp vanilla

In sauce pan heat water at medium. Stir in sugar and cornstarch; boil until mixture is clear and thick. Remove from heat; stir lemon juice and vanilla into mixture. Pour sauce over Health Cake.

Date Nut Cake

Utensils: Saladmaster Food Processor, pudding pan,
11" skillet, high dome cover, 11" utility rack,
3-qt stainless steel bowl

1	lb Graham crackers
1½	cups English walnuts
1	tsp salt
1	cup sugar
1	tsp baking powder
4	eggs; beaten
1½	cups low-fat milk
1	tsp vanilla
1	lb pitted dates; halved
4	cups water

Crush Graham crackers and chop walnuts using #1 Shredder food processor cone.

In bowl mix crackers and walnuts. Add salt, sugar and baking powder; mix well. Add eggs, milk and vanilla; mix well. Stir in dates. Pour into pudding pan.

Pour water into skillet; heat to boil at medium. Insert utility rack into skillet; place pudding pan on utility rack. Cover with high dome cover. Cook over medium heat 15 minutes. Reduce heat to low; cook 1 hour or until toothpick inserted in center comes out clean.

Serves 6-8

Carrot Cake

Utensils: Two 9" cake pans, Saladmaster Food Processor, 3-qt stainless steel bowl

3 cups grated carrots
1 cup chopped pecans
4 eggs; unbeaten
2 cups sugar
1½ cups canola oil
2 tsp baking soda
½ tsp salt
2 cups flour
2 tsp cinnamon
1 tsp vanilla

Grate carrots and chop pecans using #1 Shredder food processor cone.

In bowl combine carrots, eggs, sugar and oil; beat with electric mixer until ingredients are smooth. Add remaining ingredients; beat well. Pour batter into oiled and floured cake pans. Bake at 350° in oven 40-45 minutes. Cool; remove from pans and layer together. Ice with Cream Cheese Frosting.

Cream Cheese Frosting

Utensil: 2-qt stainless steel bowl

1 (8 oz) pkg lite cream cheese
1 lb powdered sugar

In bowl soften cheese to room temperature; blend until fluffy. Gradually beat in powdered sugar until smooth.

Apple Oatmeal Bake

Utensils: Electric skillet, 3-qt stainless steel bowl

3	large apples; unpeeled, cored, sliced ¼" thick
2	tbsp fresh lemon juice
¼	tsp ground cinnamon
⅔	cup all-purpose flour
¼	cup honey
¼	cup brown sugar; firmly packed
½	cup uncooked oatmeal
⅓	cup margarine
½	cup chopped pecans

Preheat electric skillet at 375°. Place apple slices in skillet. Sprinkle with lemon juice and cinnamon.

In bowl combine flour, honey, brown sugar and oatmeal. Cut in margarine with fork or pastry blender until mixture is crumbly. Spread over fruit. Cover; reduce heat to 250°. Bake 30 minutes or until apples are tender. Top with pecans.

Serves 6

Use this recipe with a variety of fruits for a healthy treat.

VARIATION NO. 1: In place of apples, use 6 medium fresh peaches, peeled and sliced.

VARIATION NO. 2: In place of apples, use 3 cups fresh or frozen unsweetened blueberries.

Applesauce

Utensils: 1-qt sauce pan, Saladmaster Food Processor

4	apples; unpeeled
¼	tsp ground cinnamon

Wash and core apples. Cut apples using #2 Stringer food processor cone, skin side toward cone.

Place apple in sauce pan; add cinnamon. Cook on medium heat. When Vapo-Valve "clicks," reduce heat to low. Cook 15-20 minutes. Cool.

Serves 4

Raspberry Jello Dessert

Utensils: 1-qt sauce pan, Saladmaster
Food Processor, 9" pie pan

1 (1 lb) box Graham crackers
1½ cups water
2 (3 oz) pkgs raspberry jello
2 (10 oz) boxes frozen raspberries; undrained
1 (12 oz) ctn Cool Whip

Crush Graham crackers using #1 Shredder food processor cone.

Pour water into sauce pan; boil over medium heat. Dissolve jello in water. Add raspberries. Let stand until slightly set. Cover bottom of pie pan with one-half Graham cracker crumbs. Pour in jello mixture; refrigerate until set. Top with Cool Whip and remainder of Graham cracker crumbs.

Serves 4

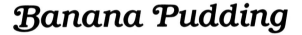

Banana Pudding

Utensils: Saladmaster Food Processor,
3-qt stainless steel bowl

3 medium bananas
½ cup lemon juice
1 (14 oz) can sweetened condensed milk
1½ cups water
1 (3½ oz) pkg instant vanilla pudding mix
2 cups whipping cream; whipped
36 vanilla wafers

Slice bananas using #3 French Fryer food processor cone. Dip slices in lemon juice.

In bowl combine milk and water. Add pudding mix; beat well. Chill 5 minutes. Fold in whipped cream. Spoon 1 cup pudding mixture into 2½-qt glass serving bowl. Top with one-third each of wafers, bananas and pudding. Repeat, layering twice, ending with pudding. Cover; chill 1 hour.

Serves 8-10

Steamed Health Pudding

Utensils: Saladmaster Food Processor, pudding pan, 3-qt sauce pan, 2-qt and 3-qt stainless steel bowls

1   cup grated potatoes
1   cup grated carrots
1   cup cut unpeeled apples; cored
1   cup chopped dates
1   cup raisins
½   cups margarine; melted
1¼ cups sugar
2½ cups flour
2   tsp salt
2   tsp baking soda
5   tsp pumpkin pie spice
4   cups water
    Nuts or cranberries (optional)

Grate potatoes and carrots and cut apples using #1 Shredder food processor cone.

Place potatoes, carrots and apples in 3-qt bowl. Add dates and raisins; mix well. Stir in margarine and sugar; mix well. In 2-qt bowl sift together flour, salt, baking soda and spice. Add to vegetable/fruit mixture; stir well. Pour batter into greased pudding pan.

Pour water into sauce pan; bring to boil at medium heat. Insert pudding pan over boiling water; steam 80 minutes. Top with nuts or cranberries, if desired.

Serves 6-8

You can use the following chart for selecting fruits:

- *1 apple - 81 calories*
- *1 banana - 105 calories*
- *1 whole grapefruit - 79 calories*
- *1 cup cantaloupe - 48 calories*
- *1 whole orange - 62 calories*
- *1 cup raisins - 496 calories*
- *2 whole plums - 72 calories*
- *1 cup grapes - 114 calories*

Puerto Rican Flan

*Utensils: 3-qt stainless steel bowl, pudding pan,
11" utility rack, electric skillet*

1   cup sugar
4   cups + 2 tbsp water
3   eggs
1   (14 oz) can condensed milk
1   (12 oz) can evaporated milk
¼   tsp salt
½   tsp vanilla

In pudding pan blend sugar and 2 tbsp of water. Heat on medium, stirring until sugar becomes brown and melts into caramel.

In bowl mix eggs and condensed milk. Add evaporated milk, salt and vanilla; blend. Pour mixture over caramel in pudding pan.

Pour 4 cups water into electric skillet; insert utility rack into skillet. Heat to boil at 225°. Place pudding pan on utility rack; steam 15 minutes or until toothpick inserted in center comes out clean. Do not overcook.

Serves 6-8

Luscious Flan on the Light Side

Utensils: 11" skillet, 11" utility rack with egg cups,
1-qt sauce pan, 2-qt sauce pan, high dome cover,
3-qt stainless steel bowl

½ cup sugar; divided
1 (12 oz) can evaporated skim milk
½ cup skim milk
¾ cup egg substitute
½ tsp almond extract
4 cups water
2 cups assorted fresh fruit

Sprinkle ¼ cup sugar in 1-qt sauce pan; place over medium heat. Cook, stirring constantly, until sugar melts and syrup is light golden brown. Pour syrup equally into six egg cups; let cool.

Pour milks in 2-qt sauce pan; heat at medium until mixture bubbles around edge of pan.

In bowl combine egg substitute, ¼ cup sugar and almond extract; beat well. Gradually add milks to egg mixture; stir constantly. Pour mixture evenly into egg cups.

Pour water into skillet; insert utility rack into skillet. Boil at medium heat. Place egg cups on utility rack. Cover with high dome cover; cook 25-30 minutes. Remove cups; chill 4 hours. To serve, loosen edges of custard; invert onto plates. Arrange assorted fresh fruit around sides.

Serves 6

Ethnic Dishes

Curried Rice

Utensils: 1-qt and 2-qt sauce pans, 1-qt stainless steel bowl

    3   cups water; divided
    1   cup uncooked long-grain rice
    ⅓   cup raisins
    2   tbsp margarine
    2   tsp curry powder
    ⅓   cup chopped walnuts; toasted

In 2-qt sauce pan bring 2½ cups water to boil. Add rice. Cover; reduce heat to low. Simmer 20 minutes or until rice is tender and water is absorbed.

In 1-qt sauce pan bring ½ cup water to boil. In bowl pour water over raisins; let stand 1 minute. Drain raisins; set aside. In 1-qt sauce pan melt margarine and add curry powder; blend. Stir curry mixture, raisins and walnuts into cooked rice.

Serves 4

Oriental Ham Soup

Utensils: 6-qt Dutch oven, Saladmaster Food Processor

    2   cups bok choy
    ¾   cup carrot strips
    ¾   cup chopped onion
    8   oz fully cooked ham
    4   cups water
    2   tbsp lite soy sauce
    2   tbsp dry cooking sherry
        Dash ground black pepper
    ½   cup spinach or egg noodles

Slice bok choy, carrots and onion using #2 Stringer food processor cone. Cut ham into thin strips.

In Dutch oven, combine water, bok choy, carrots, onion, soy sauce, sherry and pepper. Add ham and noodles. Cover; cook on medium heat until Vapo-Valve "clicks." Reduce heat to low; simmer 10 minutes or until noodles are tender and vegetables are crisp/tender.

Serves 4

Oriental Shrimp and Rice

*Utensils: 6-qt Dutch oven, 11" skillet,
Saladmaster Food Processor*

1 lb medium-size fresh shrimp
3¾ cups water
½ cup lite soy sauce
2 cups uncooked long-grain rice
1 cup chopped onion
4 tbsp margarine; divided
½ cup chopped bell pepper
4 eggs or egg substitute; beaten
⅛ tsp black pepper

Peel and de-vein shrimp; set aside.

Combine water and soy sauce in a 6-qt Dutch oven; bring mixture to boil over medium heat. Add rice. Cover; reduce heat to low. Simmer 20 minutes or until rice is tender and liquid is absorbed.

Chop onion using #2 Stringer food processor cone. Place 2 tbsp margarine in skillet; melt over medium heat. Add onion and bell pepper; saute until crisp/tender. Add shrimp; saute over medium heat 3 minutes or until shrimp is done. Spoon shrimp mixture into Dutch oven; stir into rice.

Melt remaining 2 tbsp margarine in skillet. Add eggs. Cook, without stirring, until eggs begin to set. Draw spatula across bottom of pan to form large curds. Continue until eggs are thick, but still moist. (Do not stir constantly.) Spoon eggs into rice mixture. Toss gently; season with black pepper.

Serves 6

Egg Foo Yong

Utensils: 3-qt stainless steel bowl, griddle,
Saladmaster Food Processor

¼ cup minced onion
5 eggs
½ cup chopped ham
½ lb fresh bean sprouts
½ cup chopped fresh mushrooms
1 tbsp lite soy sauce
1 tbsp canola oil

Mince onion using #1 Shredder food processor cone. Lightly beat eggs with wisk in bowl.

Add ham, onion, bean sprouts, mushrooms and soy sauce to eggs. Pour oil on griddle; heat at medium-low. Drop mixture with tablespoon into oil making small omelets. Cook until golden brown on both sides. Add more oil if needed to cook all batter. Serve with Egg Foo Yong Sauce.

Egg Foo Yong Sauce

Utensils: 1-qt sauce pan, 1-qt stainless steel bowl

1 cup chicken stock
1 tsp sugar
2 tbsp lite soy sauce
1½ tsp cornstarch
2 tbsp water

Heat stock, sugar and soy sauce in sauce pan. Mix cornstarch and water in bowl; add to stock mixture. Bring to boil; stir until slightly thick.

Serves 4

Chinese Chicken Stir-Fry

Utensils: Wok, 1-qt and 3-qt stainless steel bowls

  1 egg white
  1 tbsp dry cooking sherry
2½ tsp cornstarch; divided
  4 (3 oz) boneless, skinless chicken breast halves
  3 tbsp lite soy sauce
  1 tbsp rice wine
  2 tsp canola oil
  1 (16 oz) pkg frozen mixed vegetables (broccoli, green beans, pearl onions, red peppers)
  1 (8 oz) can bamboo shoots; drained
  1 lb fresh snow pea pods
  3 cups hot cooked rice (page 97)

Combine egg white, sherry and 1 tsp cornstarch in 3-qt bowl; beat with wire whisk until frothy. Cut chicken into thin 1" strips; add to mixture. Cover; let stand 15 minutes.

Combine soy sauce, wine and remaining cornstarch in 1-qt bowl. Beat with wire whisk; set mixture aside.

Pour canola oil into wok; heat at medium-high 2 minutes. Remove chicken from marinade. Place in wok; stir-fry 2-3 minutes. Remove chicken from wok.

Place mixed vegetables, bamboo shoots and snow peas in wok; stir-fry 3-4 minutes. Add chicken and soy sauce mixture; stir-fry until vegetables are crisp/tender. Serve over rice.

Serves 4

Chinese Hot and Sour Soup

Utensils: 3-qt sauce pan, Saladmaster Food Processor

1	small onion
4	cups chicken broth
½	cup whole straw mushrooms
½	cup bamboo shoots; halved lengthwise
¼	cup white wine vinegar
1	tbsp lite soy sauce
¼	tsp ground red pepper
6	whole black peppers
1	(12 oz) skinless pike, sea bass or sea trout fillet
1	tbsp cornstarch
1	tbsp cold water
1	egg; beaten
1	green onion; thinly sliced

Slice onion using #4 Thin Slicer food processor cone.

In sauce pan combine onion, chicken broth, mushrooms, bamboo shoots, vinegar, soy sauce, red pepper and whole peppers. Cover; cook at medium until Vapo-Valve "clicks." Reduce heat to low; simmer 5 minutes.

Measure thickness of fish. For 1"-thick fillets, cut into ½" pieces. For thinner fillets, cut into 1" pieces. Add fish to broth mixture. Return to boil; reduce heat to low. Cover; simmer gently until fish is done (allow about 2 minutes per ½" thickness).

Use slotted spoon to remove fish from soup. Cover fish to keep warm. Combine cornstarch and water; add to soup. Cook; stirring over medium heat until thick and bubbly. Cook 2 minutes.

Pour beaten egg in thin stream into hot soup. Stir gently until egg cooks and shreds finely. Remove sauce pan from heat. Gently stir in fish.

Ladle soup into individual bowls. Top with sliced green onion.

Serves 8

Middle Eastern Stew

Utensils: 4-qt roaster, Saladmaster Food Processor

½ cup chopped onion
½ cup chopped celery
2 cups sliced zucchini
3 cups water
1¼ cups (8 oz) dried lentils
2 cups 1″ cubed potatoes
2 cloves garlic; minced
1 tbsp snipped fresh parsley
1 tbsp beef bouillon granules
1 tsp ground cumin
6 lemon wedges

Chop onion and celery using #2 Stringer food processor cone. Slice zucchini using #5 Waffler cone.

Bring water and lentils to boil in roaster; reduce heat to low. Cover; simmer 30 minutes or until lentils are tender. Stir in onion, celery, potatoes, garlic, parsley, bouillon and cumin. Cover; cook 20 minutes or until potatoes are tender. Stir in zucchini. Cover; cook 10-15 minutes or until zucchini is tender. Serve with lemon wedge.

Serves 6

Stuffed Grape Leaves

Utensils: 12" casserole, 3-qt sauce pan, steamer inset, stainless steel cookie sheet, 3-qt stainless steel bowl

5	doz grape leaves; rinse thoroughly
1	lb ground beef
1	cup cooked rice (page 97)
1	tsp allspice
¼	cup fresh dill; finely cut
2	tsp fresh mint; finely cut
½	tsp tumeric
½	tsp oregano
4	cups water
1	lemon

Lay grape leaves flat on cookie sheet; set aside.

Preheat casserole at medium-high. Add ground beef; brown. Mix rice, beef and spices in bowl; blend well. Place 1 tbsp of filling in each grape leaf; fold sides in. Arrange stuffed leaves in steamer inset; alternate direction with each row.

Pour water into sauce pan; bring to boil over medium heat. Insert steamer in sauce pan. Cover; steam 20 minutes. Squeeze juice of lemon over grape leaves before serving.

Serves 10

Greek Chicken with Cinnamon

Utensils: Electric skillet, Saladmaster Food Processor, 3-qt stainless steel bowl, 8" gourmet skillet

3   small onions
6   boneless, skinless chicken breasts
½   tsp cinnamon
1   (16 oz) can tomatoes; peeled, chopped
1   (6 oz) can tomato paste
¾   cup water
2   sticks cinnamon
1   tbsp olive oil
2   cloves garlic; minced
3   cups cooked rice (page 97)
    Grated cheese

Chop onions using #2 Stringer food processor cone.

Preheat electric skillet at 375°. Place chicken in skillet. Sprinkle chicken with cinnamon; brown on both sides. Combine tomatoes, tomato paste and water in bowl; pour over chicken. Add cinnamon sticks.

Pour olive oil in gourmet skillet; heat at medium. Saute onions and garlic until tender. Add to chicken. Cover; cook at 375° until Vapo-Valve "clicks." Reduce heat to 200°; simmer 20-25 minutes. Serve over rice; sprinkle with cheese.

Serves 6

Greek Lemon Chicken

Utensils: Electric skillet, 3-qt stainless steel bowl

1   tsp garlic powder
2   tsp oregano
¼   tsp black pepper
¼   cup lemon juice
¾   cup water
3   lbs boneless, skinless chicken breasts
4   lemon slices

Combine garlic powder, oregano, pepper, lemon juice and water in bowl; stir well. Add chicken. Cover; chill 8 hours.

Remove chicken from marinade. Preheat electric skillet at 375°. Place chicken in skillet; brown on both sides. Pour marinade over chicken. Cover; reduce heat to 200°. Simmer 25 minutes or until tender. Garnish with lemon slices.

Serves 4

Greek Lamb with Green Beans

Utensils: Electric skillet, Saladmaster Food Processor

2 medium onions
2 tbsp olive oil
3 lbs lean lamb shoulder
1 (6 oz) can tomato sauce
2 lbs fresh green beans; sliced lengthwise
¼ cup chopped fresh dill
1 cup water

Chop onions using #2 Stringer food processor cone.

Pour olive oil into electric skillet; preheat at 375°. Cut lamb into 3″ cubes. Place lamb and onion in skillet; brown lamb all sides. Reduce heat to 350°. Add tomato sauce, green beans, dill and water. Cover; cook until Vapo-Valve "clicks." Reduce heat to 200°; simmer 1½ hours or until meat is tender.

Serves 6-8

Until the nineteenth century, green beans were not really an important part of the American diet. But green beans, like potatoes, traveled from the New World to Europe, where the French perfected ways to cook them.

Green beans should be picked while young and tender.

German Sauerbraten

Utensils: Electric skillet, 3-qt stainless steel bowl

- 1 cup vinegar
- 1 qt water
- 1 onion; sliced
- 3 bay leaves
- 3 cloves
- 4 lbs beef (rump, chuck, sirloin)
- 2½ tbsp canola oil
- ⅓ cup red table wine
- Cornstarch

Mix vinegar, water, onion, bay leaves and cloves in bowl. Place beef in sealable container. Pour marinade over beef. Cover; refrigerate 2-4 days. Turn twice each day.

Pour oil in electric skillet; preheat at 375°. Add meat; brown. Remove meat from skillet; set aside. In skillet add marinade reserve. Bring to boil at 375°. Add cornstarch; stir until slightly thick. Add meat. Cover; cook at 325° until Vapo-Valve "clicks." Reduce heat to 200°; cook 1-1½ hours. Add wine; cook ½ hour. Strain gravy.

Serves 8

Cuban Black Bean Soup

Utensils: 8″ gourmet skillet, Saladmaster Food Processor, 4-qt roaster

1 lb black beans
4 qts water; divided
½ lb onions; chopped
5 oz Spanish oil
½ lb bell peppers; chopped
½ tbsp oregano
5 cloves garlic; minced
½ tbsp cumin
2 tbsp white vinegar
3 cups cooked rice (page 97)

In roaster mix beans and 2-qt water. Cover; soak over night.

Drain beans; add 2-qt water. Bring to boil at medium heat. Cover; simmer 30 minutes.

Chop onions using #2 Stringer food processor cone.

In gourmet skillet heat oil at medium. Add onions and peppers; saute until tender. Add oregano, garlic, cumin and vinegar. Reduce heat to low; cook 5 minutes. Pour mixture into roaster. Cover; simmer on low heat 20-30 minutes. Serve over rice.

Serves 6

Dietary fiber is found only in plant foods. However, plant foods vary in their fiber content.

For example, cooked kidney beans have 9 fiber grams in ½ cup while ½ cup boiled green beans has 2 fiber grams.

Spanish Rice

Utensils: 11" skillet, Saladmaster Food Processor

¼ cup chopped onion
2 tbsp safflower oil
1 cup white rice
½ cup chopped bell pepper
1 clove garlic; minced
½ tsp cumin
2 cups water
1 tsp salt
⅛ tsp black pepper
1 cup chopped fresh peeled tomatoes

Chop onion using #2 Stringer food processor cone.

Pour oil in skillet; preheat at medium. Place rice in skillet; brown. Add bell pepper, onion, garlic and cumin. Saute until vegetables are tender. Add water, salt, pepper and tomatoes. Bring to boil on medium heat. Reduce heat to low. Cover; cook 20 minutes.

Serves 4

Tacoritos

Utensils: Electric skillet, 2-qt sauce pan, 9" skillet, Saladmaster Food Processor, steamer inset, 3-qt stainless steel bowl

1 cup grated Cheddar cheese
1 cup skim milk
⅛ tsp white pepper
1½ tsp chili powder
½ clove garlic; minced
2 tbsp uncooked cream of rice cereal
¼ tsp ground sage
¼ tsp dried whole oregano
¼ tsp cumin
1 tbsp minced green chili pepper
½ lb ground beef
½ cup diced onion
1 cup chopped tomato
1½ cups chopped lettuce
6 6" flour tortillas

Grate cheese using #1 Shredder food processor cone.

Combine milk, white pepper, chili powder and garlic in sauce pan. Bring to boil over medium heat. Add cereal; cook 1 minute stirring constantly. Pour into container of electric blender; process until smooth. Stir in sage, oregano, cumin and chili pepper; set aside.

Cook ground beef in 9" skillet over medium heat until brown; stir to crumble meat. Drain meat in steamer inset; pat dry with paper towel.

Combine meat, onion, tomato, and lettuce in bowl. Add ½ cup cheese and one-half sauce mixture; toss gently. Spoon ½ cup meat mixture onto each tortilla; roll and place seam side up in electric skillet. Top tortillas evenly with remaining sauce. Cover; bake at 350° for 10 minutes. Uncover; sprinkle tortillas with remaining cheese; bake additional 5 minutes.

Serves 6

Saladmaster Products

Cookware Sets

For the very best in appearance and practical utility, Saladmaster cookware is manufactured of heavy, 5-ply stainless steel. Such construction provides unequalled heat conduction for energy-saving low heat/waterless cooking . . . allowing you to retain more vital nutrition and experience less food shrinkage, providing greater value from money spent on groceries. The heat-conducting core of all Saladmaster utensils cooks food evenly. Heat from stovetop burners is rapidly transmitted throughout the multi-ply construction . . . surrounding, tenderizing and cooking food from the sides and top as well as from the bottom. Saladmaster products are available in money-saving sets or as individual cookware items, as are our accessory items and cutlery.

1½-Qt Sauce Pan
That special in-between size you've always wanted! Complements your complete cookware set.

8-Qt Roaster/Steamer
Use this roaster for both stovetop cooking and with the steamer inset for tenderizing vegetables.

10-Qt Roaster
A unit large enough to cook for a crowd. This piece is a must for those who have large families. Also available in 12-qt and 16-qt sizes.

Cook & Serve Casserole
Prepare a variety of dishes in this 12″ stainless steel casserole . . . and go directly from stovetop to table.

Griddle
Heavy gauge stainless steel perfectly cooks foods like pancakes and grilled sandwiches.

Tea Kettle
Designed for lifetime of service, this durable tea kettle features an extra thick multi-core bottom.

Wok
The gourmet delight. Stir-frying is fast, healthy and locks in natural flavors of meat and freshness of vegetables.

Accessories

Pizza Pan
Durable stainless steel won't chip or rust. Gleaming finish cleans easily and stays bright.

Electric Skillet High Dome Cover
Provides greater flexibility and space for large quantity cooking in your Saladmaster Electric Skillet.

Bake & Roast Pan
Multi-purpose pan for roasting, broiling and baking items such as large cakes, corn bread, rolls and casseroles.

Oval Baking Dish
This stainless steel baking dish is beautiful and durable. For your at-home entertaining, it will have dozens of uses.

The Gourmet Trio
A true delight for the culinary artist. 8″, 10″, 12″-skillets are best for sauteing or preparing crepes. Covers are available for all skillets.

Mixing Bowl Set
1, 2 and 3-qt stainless steel bowls are designed for use with electric mixers or wonderful for hand stirring. Ring handles provide for convenient storage.

Bakeware Set
Set includes two 9″ cake pans, two 9″ pie pans with large juice-saver rims and one cookie sheet 12½″x14½″.

Jet Coffeemaker
Automatic coffee system features modern engineered design . . . an exclusive "jet pump" for rich coffee without boiling.

Kitchen Tool Set
Made of heavy gauge metal with Russetwood handles; dishwasher safe. Convenient wall rack.

Cutlery

Saladmaster offers a complete line of fine cutlery ... designed by master craftsmen and executed in the finest stainless steel. Razor-sharp cutting surfaces feature the FIVE-STAR micro-edge, flat edge and hollow-ground edge for lasting service. Each knife is perfectly balanced for ease of use. All cutlery has Russetwood handles.

Steak Knife Set
This meat cutting set is perfect for pork chops, chicken filets or a big juicy steak. 8-piece set available with rack or "butcher block" holder.

Hunting and Filet Knife
The perfect combination for the avid hunter and fisherman. Made of 440A steel that is both sturdy and flexible to satisfy the most discriminating person.

2-Piece Stellar Set
This 2-piece set features the all-purpose kitchen shear for trimming meats and a regular paring knife.

3-Piece Apollo Set
This ensemble includes a chefs paring knife, snack knife and the 4¾" trimmer. Perfect for a gift or those smaller jobs around the kitchen.

2-Piece Vista Set
What better way to start your new cutlery collection than with a regular paring knife and a 7" carving knife.

5-Piece Satellite Set
A collection of individually designed special purpose knives: Regular paring knife, carver trimmer, butcher knife, french chef knife and 10" slicer.

3-Piece Carving Set
This beautiful carving set contains 9" carving knife with hollow-ground edge which can be sharpened to a keen razor-sharp edge. Gourmet fork, with curved shank, gives more control and strength when removing foods after cooking. The 7" carver is perfect for small roasts and hams.

Index

Breads & Desserts

Ethnic Dishes

Limited Lifetime Warranty

Saladmaster, Inc. warrants that all of our Stainless Steel Cooking Utensil products will be free from defects in material and workmanship for as long as the original retail purchaser owns the Saladmaster Stainless Steel Cooking Utensils. In the event of a malfunction or failure of a Saladmaster Stainless Steel Cooking Utensil, the purchaser should return the product, properly packaged, insured and postage prepaid to Saladmaster, Inc., Customer Service Department, 912 - 113th Street, Arlington, Texas 76010. If the malfunction or failure is a result of defects covered by this warranty, Saladmaster will, at its option, repair the Saladmaster Stainless Steel Cooking Utensil or replace it with a new Saladmaster Stainless Steel Cooking Utensil and return it to the purchaser, with charge only for transportation.

This warranty is limited to the original retail purchaser and is not transferable. The warranty does not cover damage due to accidents, neglect, abuse, tampering or misuse, nor does it cover damage resulting from service by persons other than Saladmaster.

In the event you have any questions concerning the use and care of Saladmaster Stainless Steel Cooking Utensil products or concerning service under this warranty or otherwise, please write Saladmaster, Inc., Customer Service Department, 912 - 113th Street, Arlington, Texas 76010.

Replacement Parts Service

Should a handle or knob become broken accidentally, it can be replaced for a minimum charge by writing to Saladmaster, Inc., Consumer Service Department, 912 - 113th Street, Arlington, Texas 76010. To facilitate prompt service, please identify type of replacement (long handle, side handle, cover knob).

We agree to replace your entire set of Saladmaster Cooking Utensil Products (or any part thereof) at one-half the then-current retail price at such time it is accidentally lost, stolen, destroyed or damaged by fire, flood, storm or earthquake. Proof of loss must be submitted to Saladmaster, Inc., Consumer Service Department, 912 - 113th Street, Arlington, Texas 76010 within 60 days of its occurrence.